WOMEN

AND THE

PRIESTHOOD

WHAT ONE MORMON WOMAN

BELIEVES

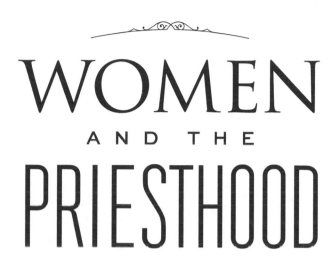

WOMEN

AND THE

PRIESTHOOD

WHAT ONE MORMON WOMAN

BELIEVES

SHERI DEW

DESERET
BOOK

SALT LAKE CITY, UTAH

DESERET BOOK is a registered trademark of Deseret Book Company.

Visit us at DeseretBook.com

Library of Congress Cataloging-in-Publication Data

(CIP data on file)
ISBN 978-1-60907-786-0

Printed in the United States of America
R. R. Donnelley, Crawfordsville, IN

10 9 8 7 6 5 4 3 2 1

CONTENTS

INTRODUCTION

Last summer I went with my mother, sisters, a sister-in-law, and several young-adult-age nieces to see a stage production of *Seven Brides for Seven Brothers* at a popular outdoor theater high in Utah's Wasatch Mountains. It was a girls' night out, and we loved being together, but the show—despite being nicely produced and featuring some fine talent—raised more than a few of my nieces' eyebrows, not to mention my own.

I'd forgotten how sexist that play was. In 1954, when the movie version of *Seven Brides for Seven Brothers* was initially released (and snagged a Best Picture nomination), the "me-Tarzan-you-Jane" way women were treated was probably considered "normal." But in the summer of 2012, the dialogue and even the plot seemed like a throwback to the Dark Ages. My nieces were uniformly bugged. Even I was surprised at the reminder of how provincial society was in its treatment and depiction of women six decades ago. I often have the same reaction when I catch an *I Love Lucy* or *Mary Tyler Moore* rerun. Though filled with unforgettable, classic humor, those golden-oldie sitcoms frequently portrayed women in stereotypical ways that elicit gasps today.

From all appearances, superficial though appearances almost always are, "we've come a long way, baby," as the old marketing slogan from the sixties goes. Some of the changes during the last half-century regarding women have been important ones—more women receiving more education, women having more protection under the law (and in some countries and cultures, for the first time), more women being compensated fairly for their work, more women benefitting from the removal of various kinds of "glass ceilings," and so on.

I am in favor of opportunities and experiences that allow for the personal development and growth of men and women alike—especially when those experiences are sanctioned by the Lord.

I am not a feminist. But I am pro-progression, meaning that I am in favor of opportunities and experiences that allow for the personal development and growth of men and women alike—especially when those experiences are sanctioned by the Lord.

By the same token, some kinds of "progress" with respect to women haven't been progress at all. Society's diminished view of motherhood and marriage as God defined them is troubling, as are the dramatic escalation of the sexualization of women in all forms of media and the ever-increasing number of out-of-wedlock births. The *Desperate Housewives, Sex and the City* approach to life that glamorizes adultery and paints immorality as normal and even desirable is alarming. And *any* trend that attempts to blur important, God-given distinctions between men and women threatens the ability of some to recognize the truth of the plan of happiness. In the clamor for women to be treated "equally" with men, many appear to have missed, misunderstood, or discarded as insignificant the innate, transcendent gifts women have been given and the unique position women have occupied in the eyes of our Creator all along.

OUR EXPERIENCES AND BELIEFS SHAPE US

As is the case with each of us, my experiences and beliefs have shaped my view of the world. I am the daughter of a Kansas grain farmer who expected me to set irrigation tubes, camp out behind the wheel of a John Deere tractor on hot summer days, and maneuver large grain trucks through the fields during harvest just like my brothers. Farm life combined with a love of sports turned me into something of a tomboy. Though I grew up in a pre-Title IX era,[1] girls' sports in the sunflower state were already big, and I never felt that my games were less important than my brothers'. At the same time, I studied the piano seriously enough to entertain the notion of becoming a concert pianist. Though I ultimately had to face the fact that I wasn't talented enough for the big leagues (on either the court or the concert stage), I did spend a stint as a pianist in a professional USO group that toured Asia, Europe, and Alaska—including a stormy flight through wind blowing sideways out to Shemya, the next-to-last island in the Aleutian chain. Through it all, my youth and young-adult years taught me that though there were certainly important distinctions between girls and boys, there was nothing constraining about *being* a girl. In fact, I deduced early on that there were significant advantages to being a girl.

In the clamor for women to be treated "equally" with men, many appear to have missed, misunderstood, or discarded as insignificant the innate, transcendent gifts women have been given and the unique position women have occupied in the eyes of our Creator all along.

From my earliest days, life has revolved around my membership in The Church of Jesus Christ of Latter-day Saints. Everything I believe about the purpose of life, the potential of eternal life, and the Atonement of Jesus Christ has been heavily influenced by prophets, seers, and revelators, by what I have learned from immersing myself in the word of

God—particularly the Book of Mormon—and by decades of regular temple worship. All I understand regarding what heaven has revealed about where women fit into the divine plan and the Lord's Church has been framed by my experience, observations, and learnings as a Latter-day Saint woman.

I will admit that I am not terribly interested in discussions about such topics as women who work versus those who don't, or the "can-women-have-it-all" debate. I am far more interested in what we know about how our Father and His Son, Jesus Christ, view and treat women. My views of this have been shaped by a body of rich doctrine as well as nearly six decades of lived experiences in which I've seen firsthand the results of the application of those truths.

Since my young-adult days, or for nearly forty years now, I've studied and prayed and thought about the place of women in the kingdom of God. In addition, it has been my privilege to meet literally millions of Latter-day Saint women around the world, and I have spent years observing, learning from, praying for, and thinking about them. Nonetheless, the initial stirrings for the combination of material in this book didn't begin until a couple of years ago. Increased attention to the Church's doctrine, practices, and the accomplishments of its members has also shined a light on LDS women. Depictions of who we are by the media have ranged from even-handed and respectful to wildly inaccurate and downright bizarre.

CAUSES OF CONFUSION

There are reasons for this. Despite frequent doctrinal declarations by Church leaders about the worth, influence, contribution, and value of women, flawed perceptions about LDS women are as old as the Church itself. Two of the causes of confusion deserve mention: first, a lingering cloud of misunderstanding over the temporary practice of polygamy, which ceased more than 120 years ago; and second, the reality that LDS women are not eligible for priesthood ordination.

First, polygamy. For a period of time during the nineteenth century, some members of the Church—a minority, actually, but among them a number of Church leaders—lived in polygamy. During the 1860s, public fervor against polygamy reached a fever pitch, and accusations that the Church degraded women flew from the halls of Congress to some state governments. Spurred largely by misunderstandings about Latter-day Saints and their beliefs, Congress passed a series of legislative acts targeting the Church, including the Morrill Anti-Bigamy Act of 1862 and the Edmunds Act of 1882, culminating with the Edmunds-Tucker Act in 1887, which, among other things, outlawed polygamous marriages. The

Despite frequent doctrinal declarations by Church leaders about the worth, influence, contribution, and value of women, flawed perceptions about LDS women are as old as the Church itself.

Church of Jesus Christ of Latter-day Saints formally renounced polygamy in 1890, and today the practice of polygamy results in swift and certain excommunication.

The second issue that has created strong opinions as well as aroused deep emotion about the Church's view of women is the fact that LDS women are not eligible for priesthood *ordination*. Hence, the purpose of this book—to explore the doctrinal question of women and the priesthood.

Because the doctrine that undergirds this vital and sensitive topic cannot be discussed in isolation from other key doctrines, the attempt of this work is to provide context and suggest a framework from which we can understand how our Father and His Son view women, as well as the privileges women have in the kingdom of God.

BEING A FEMALE IS COMPLICATED

As mentioned earlier, I love being a woman and feel there are tremendous advantages to being female. But womanhood is not uncomplicated. A woman's life is filled with ambiguity. The path for a man in the Church is somewhat laid out for him—at twelve, he'll be ordained a deacon in the Aaronic Priesthood, at fourteen a teacher, and at sixteen a priest. Then other expectations follow in short order: he will be ordained an elder in the Melchizedek Priesthood, go to the temple, enter the mission field, come home and pursue an education, find a wife and get married, earn a living, and so on. I am not suggesting that this defined path doesn't create its own stiff challenges, because it does. Our expectations—not to mention the Lord's—of believing, committed men are high and unrelenting.

A woman tends to have more flexibility than a man, but at the same time that flexibility introduces ambiguity and uncertainty. This disturbs some women. But perhaps our Father allowed this fundamental circumstance to exist to encourage women to learn to discern and follow His will. I believe that it is a reflection of His confidence in our ability to do so.

A woman's journey, however, has its own distinctive complexities. Among other things, it can be difficult to know what to prepare for. A young woman may serve a mission *if* she desires, but there is no requirement to do so. She is encouraged to get as much education as she can, but she may or may not end up using that education in some kind of professional vocation or career. And some young-adult-age women express concern that if they pursue an education or career they might be sending unintended "signals" to the Lord that they care more about a profession than about getting married. A woman should develop her talents, but how she will use them may not be clear. She may or may not marry at a traditional age. If she does marry in a "normal" time frame, she will likely desire to be a mother, but she may or may not be able to bear children. She may or may not choose to work outside the home, but in all likelihood, that decision will be charged with a variety of emotions.

In short, a woman tends to have more flexibility than a man, but at the same time that flexibility introduces ambiguity and uncertainty. This disturbs some women. *But perhaps our Father allowed this fundamental circumstance to exist to encourage women to learn to discern and follow His will.* I believe that it is a reflection of His confidence in our ability to do so.

TRUTHS I KNOW

There are risks to publishing this book, and almost daily I've been tempted to set this manuscript on a shelf and leave it there. The risks are significant:

First, I am still learning. I will understand more next year about vital Church doctrine than I know today, and more the year after, and so on. It is almost inevitable that as soon as this book goes to press, I'll hear or learn or find or come to understand something that would make a meaningful addition to this text. This is a work in progress. It seems unwise to publish something that isn't finished. But on the other hand, it will never be done.

Second, and closely associated with the first, there are plenty of things I still don't understand. Further, I could be wrong in some of my assertions. I have gone to great lengths to vet the doctrine in this book with doctrinal scholars in whom I have great confidence. Nonetheless, there may be errors in doctrinal interpretation. If there are, they are mine and mine alone.

Third, as is the case with many who put their thoughts into print for others to consider and weigh, I've taken my share of lumps. I have been judged (and in some cases harshly) plenty of times by critics for things I've said and done, and this work will likely invite criticism from various corners. Some will feel I have not gone far enough in my assertions, and others will feel I have said too much.

Fourth, today blogs and social media are filled with emotionally charged discussions about women and priesthood and Church governance. A recent major study of the attitudes of LDS women indicated that a fair number of them feel marginalized by the Church as second-class citizens. It also highlighted the fact that many women feel there is no "safe place" to share their concerns or even ask pointed questions.[2]

This is a concern. Questions are good. Questions lead to answers, as demonstrated by the Prophet Joseph Smith and countless others. The crucial issue is not about asking questions, it is the spirit in which questions are asked. A question posed against a backdrop of doubt and criticism—i.e., "I don't understand thus and such, so the Church must not be true"—can be debilitating, as it negates faith and leaves a person unable to be guided by the Spirit to learn. On the other hand, the same question asked in an environment of faith—"I don't understand thus and such, and I wonder what the Lord will teach me about that question"—demonstrates faith in the Lord and the hope that at some point an answer will be made clear. Questions asked in an environment of faith unlock the power of God to answer them.[3]

Questions asked in an environment of faith unlock the power of God to answer them.

It has not been my experience to feel marginalized in the Church, but I respect the fact that some LDS women do feel that way. Despite the significant participation that women already have in the Church (which I will say more about later), there would seem to be ways in which the visibility and legitimate involvement of women in the Church could be enhanced—and without altering doctrine, covenants, or ordinances. But ideas for change are not unique to me, nor are they unique to women.

The idea of change should neither surprise nor alarm us. Changes in policy and administration, as distinguished from doctrine, are ongoing because the Restoration is ongoing. Changes that have occurred during my lifetime would require a book of their own. We now attend Church in a three-hour block as opposed to the much different meeting schedule of my youth. There are multiple quorums of Seventy and Area Presidencies helping to administer the Church in major geographic regions around the world. More than 140 temples dot the earth, compared to a few dozen just three decades ago. Today women are much more involved in ward and stake councils than they were twenty years ago. Elders may now serve missions at age eighteen and sisters at nineteen, which change has led to a dramatic increase in the number of missionaries serving full-time missions and the number of missions in the world. And so on.

I've had far too many witnesses that the gospel is true and that the keys, power, and authority of the Savior's kingdom have been restored to let organizational issues discourage me.

Although I can see ways in which the participation of LDS women in the Church could be further enhanced, if nothing changes in my lifetime in this regard, it won't affect my testimony one whit. I've had far too many witnesses that the gospel is true and that the keys, power, and authority of the Savior's kingdom have been restored to let organizational issues discourage me.

Fifth, I could easily be misunderstood for writing this book—and probably will be. I am *not* attempting to be a spokeswoman on sensitive doctrinal issues, and I am certainly not declaring doctrine for the Church. I *do,* however, feel compelled to testify about what I know to be true. President Wilford Woodruff said that "we have nothing else to do but to build up the kingdom of God."[4] Bearing witness of the magnificent doctrine that teaches us who women are is something all converted women can do to help build this kingdom.

And finally, I have decided to publish this book, despite the risks, in an attempt to provide a different framework for the conversation about

Latter-day Saint women. Blank pages have been provided at the back of the book for readers to begin to capture their own thoughts, impressions, and learnings. My fondest hope is that this work will spur men and women alike to study, ponder, pray, discuss, and seek revelation for themselves on these life-changing, mind-expanding eternal principles.

Because the doctrine about women is glorious. It is ennobling. It is enlivening and motivating.

I love being a Latter-day Saint woman! I am grateful beyond my ability to express to know that the gospel of Jesus Christ has been restored. I am grateful for the covenants I've made that bind me to the Lord, and that bind Him to me.

I'm grateful for the direction and spiritual privileges the gospel provides, including direct access to God's power.

Attempting to live as a disciple of Jesus Christ in a world where a relative few believe in anything or anyone, let alone the Savior of the world, is seldom easy, rarely convenient, sometimes frustrating, often misunderstood, and almost never popular. But I crave the enlightenment of doctrine that answers the "whys" of life and many of the "whats" and "hows" as well. I'm grateful for the direction and spiritual privileges the gospel provides, including direct access to God's power. I am eternally indebted to the Savior for His Atonement, which is filled with healing and mercy and power for all of God's children, and I have felt His healing—including the healing that brings peace of mind—in my life more times than I can remember. I feel blessed to be alive when His gospel in its fulness is on the earth and when the priesthood has been restored. I hang on the teachings of prophets, seers, and revelators. And I love what the gospel has taught me about the exalted position of women in the eyes of the Lord—in other words, what it has taught me about who I am.

LDS WOMEN ARE INCREDIBLE

The acclaimed Western historian Wallace Stegner wrote extensively about the U.S. Western movement, including the Mormon migration. Though he did not accept the faith of the Latter-day Saints, he wrote with admiration about the courage of the Mormon pioneers—and especially the women. He said, simply, "Their women were incredible."[5]

Bathsheba Smith, who would later serve as the fourth general president of the Relief Society, is a classic example of the women Stegner honored. Describing her last moments in Nauvoo, she wrote: "We left a comfortable home, the accumulations of four years of labor and thrift and took away with us only a few much needed articles such as clothing, bedding and provisions. We left everything else behind us for our enemies. My last act in that precious spot was to tidy the rooms, sweep up the floor, and set the broom in its accustomed place behind the door. Then with emotions in my heart . . . which I then strove with success to conceal, I gently closed the door and faced an unknown future, faced a new life, a greater destiny as I well knew, but I faced it with faith in God. . . . Now I was going into the wilderness, but I was going with the man I loved dearer than my life. I had my little children. I had heard a voice, so I stepped into the wagon with a certain degree of serenity."[6]

Eliza R. Snow wrote about women in the westward company, women Stegner referred to, who "walked all day, rain or shine," rather than ride in a wagon and who then "at night prepared supper for their families, with no sheltering tents. . . . Frequently with intense sympathy and admiration I watched the mother when, forgetful of her own fatigue and destitution, she took unwearied pains to fix up in the most palatable form the allotted portion (most of the time we were rationed) of food, and as she dealt it out, was cheering the hearts of her children, while, as I truly believed, her own was lifted to God in fervent prayer that their lives might be preserved."[7]

Moral courage and faith weren't exclusive to the nineteenth century. LDS women today continue to pioneer as the gospel kingdom marches onward. Sahar Qumsiyeh, a Palestinian woman raised near Bethlehem, witnessed so much conflict and injustice in her young life that for a period of time she lost faith in God. But a scholarship to attend BYU introduced her to the Church, and when she heard President Howard W. Hunter refer to her land as "Palestine," she was intrigued. One thing led to another, and over the strong objections of her family, who claimed that "the Mormons had brainwashed her," she joined the Church.

When she moved home to the West Bank, it became an ordeal just to attend Church in Jerusalem. Because of the separation walls built to keep Palestinians on the West Bank from traveling easily or conveniently into Jerusalem, it could take hours to make the trip. Sometimes she walked for more than an hour to a place where there was a small hole in the separation wall, slipped through, and then maneuvered her way around a long line of guards. At one point in the journey she had to climb a ten-foot wall and jump down on the other side. She did this week after week. After several years of close calls and nerve-wracking trips, she obtained a United Nations job that provided the papers necessary for her to enter Jerusalem. She has subsequently served as the Jerusalem Branch Relief Society president, which carried its own unique set of challenges. Through all the upheaval, she has learned that the "only true peace has to come from the Prince of Peace Himself, our Lord and Savior Jesus Christ. The peace that the Holy Ghost brought into my life after I was baptized has remained with me during days of trouble and conflict," she testifies.[8]

Though Wallace Stegner described LDS women as incredible, I doubt Bathsheba Smith or Eliza R. Snow or Sahar Qumsiyeh saw, or see, themselves that way. And most of us living today wouldn't use that adjective to describe ourselves. I certainly wouldn't. But as an imperfect though thoroughly converted Latter-day Saint woman who is trying to live as a disciple of Jesus Christ, I declare with certainty these truths about women:

I know that women have a divine errand.

I know that God expects women to receive revelation.

I know that God is perfect and so is His Son.

I know that women are vital to the success of the Lord's Church.

I know that both women and men have access to
God's highest spiritual blessings.

I know that God reserved the high privilege of
motherhood for women.

And I know that converted women can change the world.

I do not fault anyone—in or outside the Church—for expressing contrasting views about women and the priesthood, about motherhood, and about any doctrine that cuts to the heart of who we are as women. We all speak from our knowledge and experience as well as our concerns. That is precisely what I desire to do in this book: to share what I believe heaven has revealed about the place and role of women in the Lord's Church and in the kingdom of God.

It is not possible to undertake a discussion about women and priesthood without laying a foundation that includes a discussion of such doctrinal issues as premortal existence, personal revelation, our Heavenly Father's plan, and motherhood. The chapters are arranged to provide that foundation as well as needed context.

My prayer is that what follows will either stand as a second witness to what you already know to be true or propel you forward in your own journey of spiritual discovery. May the Spirit of the Lord touch your heart and your mind, enabling you to feel and know that our identity, purpose, and value as women are shaped by an incredible body of rich doctrine that ennobles and will ultimately exalt us as covenant daughters of God.

Chapter 1

THE QUESTION OF PERCEPTION

I will never forget a meeting I attended several years ago at a major publishing house in New York City. I had been recommended to the publisher as someone who could serve as a liaison between his company and The Church of Jesus Christ of Latter-day Saints in exploring a publishing opportunity of possible interest to the Church.

About thirty minutes into our discussion, the publisher derailed the meeting when he blurted, "I just have to say that you are not what I expected." I smiled and asked what he meant, though I was fairly sure I knew what was coming next. "When I agreed to meet with a Mormon woman who is the CEO of a publishing company owned by your Church, I pictured someone quite different." When I asked what he *had* expected, he painted a fairly unflattering image, and then he repeated, "You are not what I expected."

"You might be interested to know that there are six and a half million more women just like me, if not a whole lot better," I replied. And that was when the fun for me began. I asked if he would like to know more about us, and what could he say except "yes"—after all, he had raised the topic. So with his nod, I was off and running on one of my favorite subjects: perceptions (or misperceptions, as the case may be) about Latter-day Saint women. I explained that I knew a little something about those six-plus million women, as I had met millions of them while visiting in their homes and countries when I served for five years in the Relief Society general presidency.

I then explained what the Relief Society, the Young Women, and the Primary organizations were and told him about the hundreds of thousands of LDS women worldwide serving in administrative and teaching roles on both local and general levels of Church government. I told him about the women who speak in general conference and other satellite broadcasts to worldwide audiences in 185-plus countries. I explained that LDS women have countless opportunities in the Church to lead, pray, teach, preach, and expound doctrine, including as full-time, proselyting missionaries—in other words, that we have many privileges that require ordination in other churches. I told him that roughly half of the teaching in the Church is done by women and then said that these privileges weren't recent ones prompted by political correctness, but that in 1842, long before women had many privileges under the law, the Prophet Joseph Smith had organized women in such a way that they could assume vital leadership and teaching roles in the Church. Then I told him that for years I'd searched the world over to find *any* organization—the largest governments and religions, multinational businesses, worldwide charities, major universities—where *as many women* had *as much* bona fide responsibility and authority as they

LDS women have countless opportunities in the Church to lead, pray, teach, preach, and expound doctrine, including as full-time, proselyting missionaries— in other words, we have many privileges that require ordination in other churches.

do in The Church of Jesus Christ of Latter-day Saints, and that I hadn't been able to find even one.

"Does this sound to you like a church that holds women back?" I asked.

"I had no idea," he admitted.

MISLEADING INTERPRETATIONS

The reality is that my publishing friend's perceptions are not unique. While the media are not solely to blame for perpetuating misleading perceptions, they have done their share of the damage. Three recent examples of puzzling interpretations of LDS women are representative of many others.

First: An essay in *USA Today* accused The Church of Jesus Christ of Latter-day Saints of being "hostile to the idea of female equality, let alone leadership."[1] What a curious statement about a church whose doctrine declares that a man cannot receive the highest ordinances of the temple or eventual exaltation without a woman, nor can a woman without a man. If equality means that men and women

While the media are not solely to blame for perpetuating misleading perceptions, they have done their share of the damage.

are the same, then no, we don't believe in equality. But if it means that men and women have equal access to the highest, holiest spiritual privileges, which we do, then the *USA Today* assertion shows a lack of even a cursory understanding of foundational LDS doctrine.

Second: The authors of *American Grace: How Religion Divides and Unites Us* produced one of the more credible examinations of religion in America in recent years. Nevertheless, they made several statements about Church doctrine that are misleading. They began by asserting that "while many Americans permit female clergy nowadays, there are notable exceptions across the religious spectrum, including the Catholic Church and the Mormons," then adding, "male lay leaders fill all posts in the congregational and church hierarchy."[2] They then confused the issue further by linking priesthood ordination to influence, implying that the only way to have influence is through priesthood ordination. While that linkage may be the case in other religions, it is not the case in ours.

This inaccuracy was further compounded by the statement that "entry into the pulpit (and thus positions of religious authority) has been slow"[3] among many religions. The authors of *American Grace* failed to acknowledge that Latter-day Saint women are a notable exception. LDS women have had "entry into the pulpit" for more than 170 years, preceding even the first Seneca Falls convention, where the fight for women's suffrage largely began.[4] By 1842, when the Relief Society was organized, women regularly expounded on scripture and doctrine.

Third—and my personal favorite: A female blogger writing for NYTimes.com asserted that the Church's "most distinctive characteristic" was "male authoritarianism." Seriously? Consider the implications of such a sweeping statement.

As a people, we declare without equivocation that in 1820 a fourteen-year-old boy, Joseph Smith Jr., saw God the Father and His Son Jesus Christ in a grove of trees in upstate New York, thus commencing a modern-day restoration of the Savior's own Church. This belief seems quite "distinctive." In fact, I know of no other claim by any religious organization quite like it.

We maintain that angels have played a central and recurring role in the Restoration; that the priesthood, the very power of God, was restored through heavenly messengers—first John the Baptist, followed by Peter, James, and John; that a living prophet like unto Isaiah and Daniel and the Apostle Paul walks the earth today; that the Book of Mormon: Another Testament of Jesus Christ, which was translated from ancient records delivered by an angel and which has been published in at least 82 languages with more than 160,000,000[5] copies having been printed, is scripture. All of these seem "distinctive."

At the time of this writing, the Church boasts some 75,000

missionary volunteers serving at their own expense worldwide; more than 140 temples around the globe making it possible for families to be linked eternally together; and welfare and humanitarian programs that have assisted some 30 million people in 179 countries during the last quarter century.[6] All of these facts seem at least noteworthy if not "distinctive" in their own right, but this blogger didn't as much as tip her hat to any of them.

In fact, she didn't stop there. She went on to describe the Church as a "controversial and secretive religion . . . ruled by a stern patriarchal gerontocracy" where "only 'worthy males' can ascend to positions of power—both now and in the afterlife—and women are relegated to supporting roles."[7]

What an indictment! When I read a statement such as this one, I find myself wondering if the writer has ever met, let alone talked to, a devout Latter-day Saint woman. I am talking about a card-carrying (meaning, in our case, temple-recommend-holding), tithe-paying, temple-going, actively participating woman who understands both Church government and Church doctrine. Or if she's ever visited a ward, or a Relief Society, Young Women, or Primary meeting, or the general Relief Society or general Young Women meetings broadcast by satellite around the world, or the annual BYU Women's Conference, or, for that matter, *any* women's conference in *any* stake of the Church before opining upon the role and recognition of women in The Church of Jesus Christ of Latter-day Saints.

But then, confusion—including misleading media depictions—about LDS women is nothing new. While working on President Gordon B. Hinckley's biography, I attended many press conferences where he was interviewed by diverse contingents of media. Reporters almost always posed questions that implied LDS women were second-class citizens. President Hinckley's responses were always memorable, but none more so than his statement to the National Press Club in Washington, D.C., in March 2000. After explaining that the Relief Society is one of the oldest and largest women's organizations in the world, he said: "People wonder what we do for our women. I will tell you what we do: we get out of their way and look with wonder at what they are accomplishing."[8]

WOMEN IN THE LORD'S CHURCH

LDS women have, in fact, been integral to the growth and success of the Lord's Church almost from the beginning—this despite the fact that through the annals of time, in one civilization and culture and government after another, women have typically been treated as unequals in relationship to men.

As early as 1830, Emma Smith was commanded by revelation to "expound scriptures, and to exhort the church, according as it shall be given thee by my Spirit."[9] "Exhorting the Church" implies more than an invitation—it suggests that the Lord *expected* her to preach, teach, and inspire the Saints. She was also told to give time to "writing, and to learning much." Emma was hardly relegated to a backseat. Expounding and exhorting are not assignments reserved for those on the sidelines.

LDS women have, in fact, been integral to the leadership and governance of the Lord's Church almost from the beginning.

The Lord concluded the revelation to Emma with, "Verily, verily I say unto you, that this is my voice unto *all*,"[10] making it clear that He expected not only Emma but *all* women of the Church to teach, testify, and receive spiritual gifts.

In March 1842, the Lord inspired the Prophet Joseph Smith to organize the women of the Church "after the pattern of the priesthood"[11] and to teach them "how [they] would come in possession of the privileges, blessings and gifts of the Priesthood."[12] Joseph Smith subsequently organized the Relief Society, declaring that the Church was not fully organized until the women were organized.[13] He then visited Relief Society frequently and at least six times taught the women the doctrine of the gospel, focusing particularly on priesthood, to prepare them to receive their endowment in the house of the Lord.

Because the fulness of the priesthood cannot be achieved by either a man or a woman alone, the Prophet Joseph necessarily spent time instructing the women and giving them a vision of their crucial station in the kingdom of God. Surely the day will come when Joseph Smith will be acknowledged as one of the great champions of women.

And that was just the beginning. Throughout the dispensation, Church leaders have repeatedly spoken about the honored station of women in the Lord's Church—ancient and modern, and on both sides of the veil. President Joseph F. Smith taught that the ongoing work in the spirit world is not carried on exclusively by men: "Among all these millions of spirits that have lived on the earth and have passed away . . . since the beginning of the world, without the knowledge of the Gospel—among them you may count that at least one-half are women. Who is going to carry the testimony of Jesus Christ to the hearts of the women who have passed away without a knowledge of the Gospel? Well, to my mind, it is a simple thing. These good sisters who have been set apart, ordained to the work, called to it, authorized by the authority of the Holy Priesthood to minister for their sex, in the House of God for the living and for the dead, will be fully authorized and empowered to preach the Gospel and minister to the women while the elders and prophets are preaching it to the men. The things we experience here are typical of the things of God, and the life beyond us."[14]

Because the fulness of the priesthood cannot be achieved by either a man or a woman alone, the Prophet Joseph necessarily spent time instructing the women and giving them a vision of their crucial station in the kingdom of God.

Elder Bruce R. McConkie gave insight into the role and contribution of women from the Garden of Eden forward: "Adam and Eve, Abraham and Sarah, and a host of mighty men and equally glorious women comprised that group of 'the noble and great ones,' to whom the Lord Jesus said: 'We will go down, for there is space there, and we will take of these materials, and we will make an earth whereon these may dwell' (Abr. 3:22–25). This we know: Christ, under the Father, is the Creator; Michael, his companion and associate, presided over much of the creative work; and with them, as Abraham saw, were many of the noble and great ones. Can we do other than conclude that Mary and Eve and Sarah and myriads of our faithful sisters were numbered among them? Certainly these sisters labored as diligently then, and fought as valiantly in the War in Heaven as did the brethren, even as they in like manner stand firm today, in mortality, in the cause of truth and righteousness."[15]

Elder John A. Widtsoe declared that "the place of the woman in the Church is to walk beside the man, not in front of him nor behind him. In the Church there is full equality between man and woman. The gospel, which is the only concern of the Church, was devised by the Lord for men and women alike."[16]

President James E. Faust told the women of the Church, "Surely the secret citadel of women's inner strength is spirituality. In this you equal and even surpass men, as you do in faith, morality, and commitment."[17]

And President Boyd K. Packer declared, "However much priesthood power and authority the men may possess—however much wisdom and experience they may accumulate—the safety of the family, the integrity of the doctrine, the ordinances, the covenants, indeed the future of the Church, rests equally upon the women."[18]

I could go on. Statements from prophets, seers, and revelators about the worth and stature of women are plentiful.

Indeed, we believe that our Heavenly Father created both men and women, who are His spirit sons and daughters, and that we are equal in His eyes and in the eyes of the Lord's Church. Our Father's plan is fashioned to help *anyone* who chooses to follow Him and His Son Jesus Christ achieve his or her ultimate destiny, which is to inherit eternal life.

Men and women have the *same* potential, and as free agents who can act for themselves they will either attain or lose that potential based upon the choices they make. The responsibilities, roles, and divinely endowed gifts of men and women differ in nature but not in quality, significance, or degree of importance, impact, or influence. Latter-day Saint doctrine places women equal to, and yet distinct and different from, men.

God did not intend men and women to be alike. And while He does not value either gender more than the other, President Gordon B. Hinckley put the worth of women in context when he said that as the Lord's "final creation, the crowning of His glorious work, He created woman. I like to regard Eve as His masterpiece after all that had gone before, the final work before He rested from His labors. I do not regard her as being in second place to Adam. She was placed at his side as an helpmeet. They were together in the Garden, they were expelled together, and they labored together in the world into which they were driven."[19] In another setting, President Hinckley declared that women are "the one bright shining hope in a world that is marching toward moral self-destruction."[20]

And President Thomas S. Monson told the women of Relief Society, "You are a mighty force for good, one of the most powerful in the entire world."[21]

The responsibilities, roles, and divinely endowed gifts of men and women differ in nature but not in quality, significance, or degree of importance, impact, or influence. Latter-day Saint doctrine places women equal to, and yet distinct and different from, men.

A LEGACY OF LEADERSHIP

A brief review of modern-day Church history and the place of women in it provides helpful context.

During the turbulent era when polygamy was practiced, a group of prominent LDS women spoke to a large gathering of newspaper reporters from across the country who gathered in Salt Lake City. Eliza R. Snow, then general president of the Relief Society, declared that "it was high time [to] rise up in the dignity of our calling and speak for ourselves. . . . The world does not know us, and truth and justice to our brethren and to ourselves demands us to speak. . . . We are not inferior to the ladies of the world, and we do not want to appear so."[22] Afterwards, a reporter from the *New York Herald* summed the reaction of many in attendance: "In logic and rhetoric the so-called degraded ladies of Mormondom are quite equal to the . . . women of the East."[23]

In point of fact, Latter-day Saint women have always been able to hold their own. The doctrine and practices of the Church regarding women give us confidence born of the Spirit and teach us how to lead, teach, testify, rally others to a worthy cause, and express ourselves. And it has always been so.

The doctrine and practices of the Church regarding women give us confidence born of the Spirit and teach us how to lead, teach, testify, rally others to a worthy cause, and express ourselves. And it has always been so.

In 1870, women living in the Utah Territory were granted the right to vote by the territorial legislature. In sharp contrast to the long fight for women's suffrage nationally, the vote came to Utah women with nominal effort on their part. The Edmunds-Tucker act subsequently disenfranchised women in the Utah Territory, but the voting right was restored in 1896 when women's suffrage was written into the constitution of the new state of Utah. In Utah's first election following statehood, Martha Hughes Cannon, a Democrat, became the first woman in the U.S. to win a seat in a state senate, which she did by defeating her Republican husband, Angus, for that seat.

In 1868, Church President Brigham Young not only emphasized

both vocational and professional education for women but applauded the admission of women to the University of Deseret in Salt Lake City. He encouraged women to become writers, poets, and physicians—and many did. His words led to the establishment of the *Woman's Exponent,* a semimonthly periodical written by and for LDS women. And his encouragement that "a good many [sisters] . . . get a classical education, and then a degree for Medicine" prompted Romania B. Pratt, Ellis and Margaret Shipp, and Martha Hughes (Cannon), among others, to go east to medical school and become physicians.[24]

Nineteenth-century LDS women showed leadership in other ways as well.

Both the Relief Society and Young Ladies Mutual Improvement Association[25] became charter members of the International Council of Women in 1888 and its U.S. affiliate, the National Council of Women, in 1891. In March 1888, Emily S. Richards spoke to the First International Council of Women, reporting on the activities of 22,000 members of 400 local Relief Societies. Her remarks paint a picture of the scope of Relief Society at that time: "They own many of the halls in which they meet, and such property is valued at $95,000. They have laid up wheat in granaries to the amount of 32,000 bushels, for seed or relief in case of scarcity. They assist in caring for the distressed, help to wait upon the sick and prepare the deceased for burial. . . . The Deseret Hospital, with a lady M.D. as Principal, and skilled nurses and attendants, is under their direction. They have fostered the silk industry, producing the raw material and manufacturing it into various articles. They encourage industry as well as intellectual culture. . . . [Relief Society's] benefits are felt in every place where it extends, all its tendencies being to make women useful, progressive, independent, and happy."[26]

When in 1876 President Young charged Emmeline B. Wells with leading an effort among the Church's women to store grain against a time of famine, he admitted that "the men have tried for years, but they have continued to let the grain go; now we want to see if the sisters will be more successful."[27] They had all kinds of problems storing the wheat. It got moldy and filled with weevils. Thousands of bushels were lost as they experimented. But the women persisted. Over the decades, they learned to raise money to buy wheat, to raise wheat themselves, to store it properly, and to mill it into flour. Not only would their efforts be successful, over time they would pay dividends. After San Francisco's devastating 1906 earthquake, the first carload of flour to reach the survivors was from wheat milled from Relief Society reserves. The following year, the Relief Society sent wheat to China to help with a famine there. And most notably, during a worldwide grain shortage that complicated troop logistics during World War I, the Relief Society sold some 200,000 bushels of grain to the U.S. government.[28]

The Relief Society's wheat contribution was deemed significant enough that after the war's end, President and Mrs. Woodrow Wilson visited Salt Lake City, in part to thank Emmeline B. Wells, the Relief Society general president, for the wheat that had helped keep troops alive during the war.

Herbert Hoover, then head of the U.S. Food Administration, wrote to Utah Congressman Milton H. Welling: "The recent action of the women of the Church of Jesus Christ of Latter-day Saints, in Utah, in releasing wheat and flour for the use of our allies and our own soldiers abroad is so commendable that I wish to drop you this line merely to assure you of my appreciation of this service performed by the Church."[29] The Relief Society's wheat contribution was deemed significant enough that after the war's end, President and Mrs. Woodrow Wilson visited Salt Lake City, in part to thank Emmeline B. Wells, the Relief Society general president, for the wheat that had helped keep troops alive during the war.

On the other side of the Atlantic, Ida Bowman Smith accompanied her husband, Elder Hyrum Mack Smith of the Quorum of the Twelve, to

England in 1913, where he presided over the Church's European Mission during World War I. Ida worked tirelessly to organize Relief Societies throughout England to help with the war effort. Those sisters rolled bandages, made mittens, and knitted socks—hundreds of thousands of them. At the war's end, Ida was recognized by the Lady Mayoress of Liverpool and received a citation from the English government and a medal from the king and queen of England for her efforts.[30]

Eliza, Emmeline, Ida, and countless other women from the Church's earliest days have exemplified Brigham Young's view that women have "an immense amount of influence in guiding, directing, and controlling human affairs."[31]

WOMEN OF THE CHURCH TODAY

It is not just the women of yesteryear who have come through valiantly in keeping their covenants and living as women of God.

For decades now I have had the privilege of meeting, worshiping with, and learning from the women of this Church—women who look and act like followers of Jesus Christ. I have met them in the sweltering heat and humidity of the Amazon and the frigid, forbidding winter of Siberia. Again and again, I have seen women who have the faith to move mountains and the moral courage to confront evil masquerading as enlightenment. These are women who, as Elder D. Todd Christofferson described, "can persevere against hardship, who can sustain hope through tragedy, who can lift others by their example and their compassion, and who can consistently overcome temptations."[32]

Again and again, I have seen women who have the faith to move mountains and the moral courage to confront evil masquerading as enlightenment.

One such group of women lives in Christchurch, New Zealand, where a few years ago they suffered three major earthquakes within a matter of months, one of them measuring 7.1 in magnitude, and more than eight thousand aftershocks, sometimes as many as twenty a day. One hundred eighty-two individuals lost their lives in those quakes, more than a thousand homes were damaged or destroyed, and nearly everyone in Christchurch lost something or someone.

A member of the Christchurch Parliament acknowledged that many times it was Church members, both men and women, who stepped forward to help with difficult challenges—providing homes for and feeding the homeless, dispensing water, helping with first aid, and working non-stop to care for children, make meals, distribute bedding and clothing, clear debris, or comfort the forlorn. "Christchurch is going to be able to rebuild," the Parliamentarian said, "and it is things like what the LDS Church has done that has brought our community together."

Melanie Riwai-Couch, an LDS woman in Christchurch who at one point during the earthquakes' aftermath wrote her infant daughter's name and address on her blanket in case she became separated from the family, articulated the attitude and strength of her sister Saints in Christchurch: "The most important thing I have learned through all of this is that you can be prepared, but at the end of the day, it is in God's hands. If we die, we die. The only thing we can do is to be doing everything we can to honor the covenants we have made. And then, we might be ordinary women but we have an extraordinary ability to be a force for good in our homes and our communities. That is the legacy of Relief Society."[33]

And it is the legacy of women of God today.

Eliza R. Snow asserted that "although the name [of Relief Society] may be of modern date, the institution is of ancient origin. We were told

To view a video segment featuring the women of Christchurch and how they responded to this crisis, scan this code or visit **seek.deseretbook.com/christchurch.**

by our martyred prophet that the same organization existed in the church anciently."[34]

In organizing the women of the Church by establishing the Relief Society, the Prophet Joseph Smith signaled the restoration of an ancient pattern—a pattern in which women are vital to the onward march of the kingdom of God.

Chapter 2

WOMEN HAVE
A DIVINE ERRAND

In an interview taped in December 1995 for a segment that later appeared on CBS's *60 Minutes,* veteran journalist Mike Wallace asked President Gordon B. Hinckley if he believed in an afterlife. President Hinckley caught Wallace off guard when he responded, "I certainly do. I think life after this life is as certain as life here. I believe we lived before we came here, that we live for a purpose . . ."

"Wait. Wait," Wallace interrupted. "You believe we lived *before* we came here?"

"Oh absolutely, as intelligences, as spirits," President Hinckley replied.

"There was a spirit of Gordon Hinckley?" Wallace asked.

"Absolutely, and of Mike Wallace."

"I hope not," Wallace joked.

"Life is an eternal thing, Mike," President Hinckley continued. "It is part of an eternal plan, our Father's plan for His sons and daughters, whom He loves. His work and His glory is to bring about the immortality and eternal life of His sons and daughters. It has purpose. It has meaning."[1]

Mike Wallace wasn't and isn't the only person intrigued with the notion of our having lived before we came here and the potential of our living beyond the grave. Poets and philosophers have mused about who we are, where we came from, why we are here, and where we're going for as long as records have been kept and words have been written.

Plato, widely regarded as the father of Western philosophy, believed that our principle objective as mortals was "becoming like god so far as is possible." Where other ancients regarded such talk as blasphemy, he believed that seeking to become like God honored rather than diminished Him.[2]

Early Christian writers such as Irenaeus, writing in the second century, opined upon our divine destiny: "We have not been made gods from the beginning, but at first merely men, then at length gods."[3]

Modern theologian C. S. Lewis went even further, writing that "the Church exists for nothing else but to draw men into Christ, to make them little Christs. If they are not doing that, all the cathedrals, clergy, missions, sermons, even the Bible itself, are simply a waste of time. God became Man for no other purpose. It is even doubtful . . . whether the whole universe was created for any other purpose."[4]

Plato believed that seeking to become like God honored rather than diminished Him.

And then, there is C. S. Lewis's oft-quoted statement that "it is a serious thing to live in a society of possible gods and goddesses, to remember that the dullest and most uninteresting person you talk to may one day be a creature which . . . you would be strongly tempted to worship. . . . It is in light of these overwhelming possibilities, it is with the awe and circumspection proper to them, that we should conduct all our dealings with one another. . . . There are no ordinary people. You have never talked to a mere mortal."[5]

Perhaps nothing affects our ability to become who we're capable of becoming more than does knowing who we are, who we have always been, how *real* our divine potential is, and that we each have a divine errand[6]—meaning, that we have come to this earth with a mission to perform. Our errands are all different. Your life's mission is not mine, and mine is not yours. They are all the same in their origin, however. They came from God.

President Spencer W. Kimball taught that "in the world before we came here, faithful women were given certain assignments while faithful men were foreordained to certain priesthood tasks. While we do not now remember the particulars, this does not alter the glorious reality of what we once agreed to. You are accountable for those things which long ago were expected of you just as are those we sustain as prophets and apostles!"[7]

> *Our errands are all different. Your life's mission is not mine, and mine is not yours. They are all the same in their origin, however. They came from God.*

Because of the commitments we made premortally, we are most likely to enjoy peace of mind, to be happy, and to be able to serve and have influence when the course we are pursuing is in harmony with those promises. This requires earnest effort to uncover and fulfill our divine errand. First and foremost in this quest is understanding who we are and how our Father sees us.

As a people, we talk and sing constantly about this. Three-year-olds know the words to "I Am a Child of God." "The Family: A Proclamation to the World" declares that we each have a divine destiny. And every week in thousands of congregations across the earth, teenage girls stand and recite the Young Women theme, which begins, "We are daughters of our Heavenly Father, who loves us, and we love Him." And yet, with all our singing and talking, do we really believe? Do we really understand the implications? Has this transcendent doctrine about who we are—meaning who we have always been and, therefore, who we may become—penetrated our sense of identity?

Our spirits long for us to remember the truth about who we are because the way we see ourselves affects everything we do. It affects how we treat others, how seriously we work to develop ourselves and progress, how we handle both success and defeat, how we feel about the Lord Jesus Christ and His message, and whether or not we are more interested in *this* life or life forever.

> *Our spirits long for us to remember the truth about who we are because the way we see ourselves affects everything we do.*

There is a lesson to be learned from the Apostle Paul about the impact of understanding who we are. Prior to Paul's conversion, when he was known as Saul, he had turned the persecution of Christians into an art form, "breathing out threatenings and slaughter against the disciples of the Lord."[8] Upon seeing the Savior and being told that he was a "chosen vessel," Saul was instantly converted.[9] And yet, no Christian who had felt the wrath of Saul of Tarsus would have described him as "chosen." In fact, when the Lord instructed Ananias to administer to Saul, his initial reaction was, "Isn't that the man who has done so much evil to the Saints in Jerusalem?"[10] But Saul had been chosen before, *premortally.* And when Saul understood that—when he understood that he was living for more than himself—he changed not only his name but his life. Part of the Apostle Paul's conversion was coming to understand who he was, who he had always been, and that he had a divine errand.

Just as Saul had a divine errand, so do we.

THE MOST INSPIRING OF ALL CAUSES

It is actually easier to motivate someone to do something difficult than something easy. That truth may seem counterintuitive, but it shouldn't. Our spirits crave to progress, and if we aren't moving forward, we're not happy. The plan of happiness is pro-progression; thus the desire to progress is hardwired into our divine DNA. Whether we're conscious of it or not, we crave the feeling of moving forward, learning, growing, and improving—even if our steps forward are small and intermittent. That is why the lack of even modest progress leads to disillusionment and discouragement, whereas steady progress instills peace of mind and optimism.

How inspiring would it be if our Father had said, "Be ye therefore mediocre"? Though our knees buckle at times under life's burdens, and though we tend to flinch when talking or thinking about aspiring to perfection, none of us wants to stay just like we are. Embedded within our spirits is the need to become more and more like our Father and His Son.

The plan of happiness is pro-progression; thus the desire to progress is hardwired into our divine DNA. Whether we're conscious of it or not, we crave the feeling of moving forward, learning, growing, and improving.

This truth regarding our innate need to progress crystallized for me several years ago when the publishing team at the company where I work announced their goal to place three books on the *New York Times* best-seller list. I said, "Terrific!" and walked back to my office thinking, "Zero chance." In our company's 140 years, we hadn't charted a single book on that list. But the team developed and executed a smart plan and actually put not three but four books on the *New York Times* list that year. They were highly motivated by the prospects of accomplishing something they had never done before. They caught the vision of what they could do and rallied to a difficult but inspiring cause.

The most demanding but inspiring of all causes is doing what we came to this earth to do and becoming who we have the potential of becoming.

Norman Cousins, an American journalist and author, asserts that "the human potential is the most magical but also most elusive fact of life. Men suffer less from hunger or dread than from living under their moral capacity. The atrophy of spirit that most men [and women] know and all men [and women] fear is tied not so much to deprivation or abuse as it is to their inability to make real the best that lies within them. Defeat begins more with a blur in the vision of what is humanly possible than with the appearance of ogres in the path."[11]

Sometimes we let our insecurities, lack of vision, and other weaknesses get in the way of developing the best that lies within us. Elder Jeffrey R. Holland used strong language in counseling us about how to deal with our limitations: "If you lack confidence or always sound apologetic or feel you have an inferiority complex, *get over it*. We all start humbly, . . . we all think the fellow seated on our right and the woman seated on our left are more talented, are more gifted, . . . and are going to do better in life than we ever will. Well, they aren't, and they don't, and they won't! They are just like you. We all have our fears and insecurities. . . . But it would be fatal to stay in that swamp of insecurity, to mire down and stop, to fail to look up and fail to look ahead and fail to be believing."[12]

The most demanding but inspiring of all causes is doing what we came to this earth to do and becoming who we have the potential of becoming.

THE CHALLENGE TO LOOK UP

Looking up, which includes seeking a spiritual witness from God, is the only way to understand who we are. The world is utterly incapable of giving us an accurate view of ourselves. We don't just hope for a glorious future, we believe it's actually possible to "dwell with God in a state of never-ending happiness."[13] This is because those who understand our Heavenly Father's plan of happiness for His children think differently than those who don't know about, understand, or believe in that plan. For example, I recently attended a young single adult ward in Sydney, Australia, where a beautiful young woman bearing her testimony said simply, "I know I am a child of God and am special, even if I'm a nobody in the world."

Because of the teachings and writings of prophets through the millennia, those who do believe in Heavenly Father's plan know that God the Father is literally the Father of our spirits.[14] Jehovah made this clear when He declared, "Ye are gods; and all of you are children of the most High."[15] Our Father knows us by name and by attribute. He watched us grow and learn, make choices and progress premortally. He knows our hearts, our weaknesses and strengths, the spiritual gifts He's given us, and our potential. He knows what we were foreordained to do here on earth. He hears our prayers and understands our anguish and insecurities. He loves us completely and perfectly.

Our Father knows us by name and by attribute. He watched us grow and learn, make choices and progress premortally. He knows our hearts, our weaknesses and strengths, the spiritual gifts He's given us, and our potential.

The Apostle Paul taught the Romans that "the Spirit itself beareth witness with our spirit, that we are the children of God: And if children, then heirs; heirs of God, and joint-heirs with Christ."[16] Paul carried that theme into his letter to the Philippians, declaring, "I press toward the mark for the prize of the high calling of God in Christ Jesus."[17] In short, the Apostle Paul was aiming for godhood and urging all he taught to do the same.

Lorenzo Snow declared that "Jesus was a god before he came into the world and yet his knowledge was taken from him. He did not know his former greatness, neither do we know what greatness we had attained to before we came here, but he had to pass through an ordeal, as we have to, without knowing or realizing at the time the greatness and importance of his mission and works."[18]

But President Snow also taught that during the Savior's life "it was revealed unto Him who he was, and for what purpose He was in the world. The glory and power He possessed before He came into the world was made known unto Him."[19]

Just as the Savior came to understand who He was, so may we.

President Joseph F. Smith explained that the divinity within us responds to whisperings of the Spirit about who we are and who we have always been: "In coming here, we forgot all, that our agency might be free indeed, to choose good or evil, that we might merit the reward of our own choice and conduct. But by the power of the Spirit, in the redemption of Christ, through obedience, we often catch a spark from the awakened memories of the immortal soul, which lights up our whole being as with the glory of our former home."[20]

There is a direct connection between our premortal lives and life here. Elder Dallin H. Oaks explained: "We had progressed as far as we could without a physical body and an experience in mortality. To realize a fulness of joy, we had to prove our willingness to keep the commandments of God in a circumstance where we had no memory of what preceded our mortal birth. . . . Many of us also made covenants with the Father concerning what we would do in mortality. In ways that have not been revealed, our actions in the spirit world influence us in mortality."[21]

This life really isn't about this life. It is about what comes next.

Mortality is a brief but vitally important stage in this eternal journey designed to help us ultimately become like our heavenly parents. It is a period of testing, a season of probation. When our lives are finished, we will again step across a veil—this time the veil that separates this world from the next. Life here on this earth is not an end in and of itself. It is a crucial step in our eternal progression.[22]

Thus, this life really isn't about this life. It is about what comes next.

THE IMPACT OF OUR PREMORTAL LIFE

Understanding who we are would be easier if we could remember our premortal life. But we can't. We can't remember the glory of our former home—which is just as well, for we would "pine for it," as President George Q. Cannon explained.[23] We have forgotten the language we spoke there and our dear companions with whom we associated. We cannot recall the "first lessons [we learned] in the world of spirits" or the identities of our heavenly tutors.[24] We can't remember what promises we made to ourselves, to others, and to the Lord. Nor can we remember our place in the Lord's heavenly kingdom or the spiritual maturity we reached there.[25]

There are, however, some remarkable things we *do* know. We know that *we were there,* in the heavenly councils before the foundations of this earth were laid. We know that *we were there* when our Father presented His plan and the Savior was chosen and appointed to be our Redeemer—and, as the Prophet Joseph Smith taught, we "sanctioned it."[26] *We were there* among the heavenly host who sang and shouted for joy.[27]

We know that throughout premortality we had the agency to make our own choices, and that those choices affect us in this life. Said President Joseph Fielding Smith: "God gave His children their free agency even in the [premortal] spirit world, by which the individual spirits had the privilege, just as men have here, of choosing the good and rejecting the evil, or partaking of the evil to suffer the consequences of their sins. Because of this, some even there were more faithful than others in keeping the commandments of the Lord. . . . The spirits of men had their free agency. . . . The spirits of men were not equal. They may have had an equal start, and we know they were all innocent in the beginning; but the right of free agency which was given to them enabled some to outstrip others, and thus, through the eons of immortal existence, to become more intelligent, more faithful, for they were free to act for themselves, to think for themselves, to receive the truth or rebel against it."[28]

We also know that when Satan rebelled against the Father and the Son and was cast out of heaven, we made the most crucial choice of our premortal lives when we chose to fight on the side of truth.[29] In fact, President George Q. Cannon said that "we stood loyally by God and by Jesus, and . . . did not flinch."[30] We were believers, and we stood firm.

When we were born, we "graduated" from that premortal life. William Wordsworth wrote of this with these now-famous lines:

> Our birth is but a sleep and a forgetting:
> The Soul that rises with us, our life's Star,
> Hath had elsewhere its setting,
> And cometh from afar:
> Not in entire forgetfulness,
> And not in utter nakedness,
> But trailing clouds of glory do we come
> From God, who is our home.[31]

Now we are here, separated from the safety of our heavenly home, each of us serving a mission in this wilderness called mortality—a mission to prove whether or not we want to be part of the kingdom of God (both here and hereafter) more than we want anything else. The Lord is testing our faith, our integrity, and our desires to see if we will persevere in a realm where Satan reigns. Happily, despite taking this test in the stormy twilight of the dispensation of the fulness of times, we have once again chosen to follow Christ. The Lord was speaking of His followers when He said, "My sheep hear my voice, . . . and they follow me."[32] Those who hear His voice do so because they *remember* and *recognize* His voice and the voice of His servants.[33]

As Elder Tad R. Callister has written,

The Lord is testing our faith, our integrity, and our desires to see if we will persevere in a realm where Satan reigns. Happily, despite taking this test in the stormy twilight of the dispensation of the fulness of times, we have once again chosen to follow Christ.

"The purpose of this earth life is to serve as a probationary estate, to see if we will repent and follow Christ."[34] It is as simple, and as rigorous, as that.

NOBLE AND GREAT

We are among the elect whom the Lord has called during this "eleventh hour" to labor in His vineyard, a vineyard that "has become corrupted every whit" and in which only a few "doeth good."[35] We are those few.

God, who saw "the end from the beginning,"[36] foresaw perfectly what these times would demand. President George Q. Cannon repeatedly taught that God reserved his "noblest spirits" to come forth in this last dispensation.[37] "God has chosen us out of the world and has given us a great mission," he said. "I do not entertain a doubt myself but that we were selected and fore-ordained for the mission before the world was; that we had our parts allotted to us in this mortal state of existence as our Savior had his assigned to him."[38] Further, he declared that the Lord saved for now those spirits who would have "the courage and determination to face the world and all the powers of the evil one," and who would nonetheless "build up the Zion of our God fearless of all consequences."[39]

The Lord told Abraham that he was among the "noble and great ones" chosen for his earthly mission before he was born.[40] And in a vision that was subsequently canonized, President Joseph F. Smith saw that *many* choice spirits reserved to come forth in this dispensation were "among the noble and great."[41]

Is it possible that we were among the noble and great? I believe it is more than possible.

Surely our Father, who has inspired prophets from the beginning of time to prophesy about what would happen in this culminating dispensation when "nothing shall be withheld,"[42] would not have taken a chance on the outcome of the last days by sending men and women he couldn't count on.

I cannot imagine that we who have been called to bear and rear and love and lead a chosen generation of children and youth this late in the final dispensation were not among those deemed noble and great.

Noble and great. Courageous and determined. Faithful and fearless. That is who we are, and it is who we have always been.

I doubt many of us feel noble or great. But then neither did Enoch, who was stunned when the Lord called him into service: "Why is it that I have found favor in thy sight, and am but a lad, and all the people hate me; for I am slow of speech . . . ?"[43] The Lord responded to Enoch by promising to walk with him and give power to his words. Surely this encounter with the Lord gave Enoch a new vision of himself. And the result was magnificent, for so powerful was his word that his people were "taken up into heaven."[44] But it happened *after* Enoch understood who he was and that he had a mission to perform.

As we come to understand the same thing, we will feel greater purpose and more confidence living as women of God in a world that doesn't celebrate women of God. We will cheer each other on rather than compete with each other, because we will be looking for validation from the Lord rather than from the world. And we will be willing to stand for truth, even when that means standing alone.

> *Surely our Father, who has inspired prophets from the beginning of time to prophesy about what would happen in this culminating dispensation, would not have taken a chance on the outcome of the last days by sending men and women he couldn't count on.*

ONE OF THE LORD'S MOST EFFECTIVE WEAPONS

Satan of course knows how spiritually potent the knowledge of our divine identity is. He hates women of the noble birthright. He hates them because he is almost out of time. He hates them because of the influence we have on husbands and children, family and friends, the Church and even the world. It is no secret to him that covenant-keeping women are one of the Lord's most effective weapons against his sinful, sinister strategies.

On this point, a passage from Revelation is illuminating. We learn that Michael and angels fought against Satan, and Satan and his angels were cast out. "Woe to the inhabiters of the earth," we are warned, "for the devil is come down unto you, having great wrath, because he knoweth that he hath but a short time." Satan is cast out, is furious, and is out for revenge and destruction—and he knows he has only a short time to wreak his havoc. Then comes the chilling prophecy that Satan will "[persecute] the woman which brought forth the man child. . . . The dragon was wroth with the woman, and went to make war with the remnant of her seed, which keep the commandments of God, and have the testimony of Jesus Christ."[45]

The Joseph Smith Translation of this passage from John the Revelator indicates that "the woman" is symbolic of the Church. But I cannot read this passage without thinking about it literally. From the beginning of time, women have been one of Satan's principal targets. He has done everything within his considerable power to abuse and oppress women, entice and seduce women, encourage women to seduce men, convince women that their only value is the sexuality of their bodies, confuse women with the ambiguities and uncertainties that seem to swirl around our gender, and through it all to keep women from comprehending the majesty of who they are and the plain fact that the plan of salvation is utterly dependent upon a woman's primary role, the privilege of bearing and rearing children (more on this in chapter 7).

Consider the way the world regards the two greatest women to have ever lived—Eve and Mary. For the central, life-giving role she played in the Garden of Eden, Eve has been vilified and accused of everything from weakness to immorality. Mary, on the other hand, has been worshiped for bearing the Christ child. Both reactions are distorted. We don't worship either woman, but we revere both for their unparalleled roles in helping make the plan of salvation a reality—Eve for setting in motion the process by which every one of us progresses from premortality to mortality, and Mary for being worthy and willing to bear and rear the Savior.

Today opinions about women run the gamut. Recently, one prominent executive of a multibillion-dollar company implored women in a *New York Times* best-selling title to "Lean In" to their careers and ascend in business as high as possible rather than make children or family a priority. At the same time, another female executive, a former CFO of a global financial services firm and at one time one of the most powerful women in finance, said in a widely broadcast interview that the price she had paid to rise to the top of the male-dominated Wall Street world was too high, that she regretted not having children, and that women shouldn't follow in her footsteps.[46]

From time immemorial, controversies and distortions have swirled around women. Consider a recent study from the University of Southern California, home of one of the top-rated film schools in the United States, which confirmed what everyone who has stepped inside a movie theater during the last few decades already knew—that the movie industry sexualizes women to sell tickets. "The data speaks to an overemphasis on beauty, thinness, and sexualization of women at younger and younger ages," the study reported. "These findings are troubling given that repeated exposure to thin and sexy characters may contribute to negative effects in some female viewers."[47]

Count on it.

Satan wants us to see ourselves as the world sees us, not as the Lord sees us. Every time I have spoken in general Church meetings broadcast on satellite, I have received letters commenting on everything from my clothes to the speed at which I spoke. One favorite letter said, "Sister Dew, I can relate to you because I can see that you know what it is to have a bad-hair day." I've had years of bad-hair days, so that letter made me laugh. But I can't help but wonder if men receive the same comments about the color of their ties or their haircuts.

We don't always see beyond our hair and our clothing, but the Lord does. For He "seeth not as man seeth; for man looketh upon the outward appearance, but the Lord looketh on the heart."[48]

Satan's superficialities, distractions, and distortions are an all-out attempt to confuse and derail women, to confuse men about women, and to prevent all from understanding how the Lord views His daughters. Confusion about our identity can wreak havoc. But clarity about who we are is empowering.

The more clearly we understand our divine destiny, the more immune we become to Satan.

When Satan tried to confuse Moses about his identity, saying, "Moses, *son of man,* worship me," Moses refused, responding: "I am a *son of God.*" He knew who he was because the Lord had told him, "Thou art my son; . . . and I have a work for thee."[49] The great deceiver ranted and railed, but Moses prevailed because he knew who God was, and he knew that he, Moses, was His son.

The more clearly we understand our divine destiny, the more immune we become to Satan.

So it is with us. We will never be happy or feel peace; we will never deal well with life's stresses and ambiguities; we will never live up to who we are as women of God unless we overcome our mortal identity crisis and understand who we have always been and who we may become. The truth about who we are and who we have always been carries a sense of purpose that cannot be duplicated in any other way. This is because, as Elder Callister explained, "with increased vision comes increased motivation."[50]

And the vision of who we may become is spectacular. "All Israel," wrote Elder Bruce R. McConkie, "have it in their power to gain exaltation; to be like the Son of God, having gained his image; to be joint-heirs with him; to be justified and glorified; to be adopted into the family of God by faith; to be participators with their fathers in the covenant that

God made with them; and to be inheritors . . . of the ancient promises. Implicit in all this is the fact that they are foreordained to be baptized, to join the Church, to receive the priesthood, to enter the ordinance of celestial marriage, and to be sealed up unto eternal life."[51]

THE LONG HEREAFTER VERSUS THE BRIEF PRESENT

Though we sometimes get distracted by the world and live beneath ourselves—though we are sometimes too casual about our spiritual lives—the fact remains that *we have always been daughters of God.* We chose to follow Jesus Christ premortally, and we have chosen to follow Him again. For all of our weaknesses, for all the times we know that we fall short of the standard our Father has set for us, we have *repeatedly* made righteous choices, on both sides of the veil, that demonstrate our desire to be followers of Jesus Christ. We have done this by binding ourselves to the Lord with the most binding covenants of mortality.

We are not here by chance, the result of some undefinable Big Bang that miraculously resulted in an earth where the ecosystem magically works and where people gradually evolved from some lower life form into who we are today. Before we came here, we lived as spirits with God, our Father. We knew Him, and He knew us—individually and by name.

For all of our weaknesses, for all the times we know that we fall short of the standard our Father has set for us, we have repeatedly *made righteous choices, on both sides of the veil, that demonstrate our desire to be followers of Jesus Christ.*

President Ezra Taft Benson declared that "nothing is going to startle us more when we pass through the veil to the other side than to realize how well we know our Father and how familiar His face is to us." Then, paraphrasing Brigham Young, he added that we're likely "going to wonder why we were so stupid in the flesh."[52]

45

Eternity awaits. *Our* eternity—meaning what quality of life we have forever—will be a direct reflection of the choices we make and the way we spend our time here on earth. The Roman philosopher Cicero declared that he was far more interested in the "long hereafter than the brief present."[53] And President Spencer W. Kimball promised that "the more clearly we see eternity, the more obvious it becomes that the Lord's work in which we are engaged is one vast and grand work with striking similarities on each side of the veil."[54]

In short, what we do with our lives matters. As Gandalf, a character in J.R.R. Tolkien's *Lord of the Rings* trilogy, said, "All we have to decide is what to do with the time that is given us."[55]

The Savior told us how to spend that time when He commanded us to become as He is. President Joseph Fielding Smith explained why this does not have to seem overwhelming: "I believe the Lord meant just what he said: that we should be perfect, as our Father in heaven is perfect. That will not come all at once, but line upon line, and precept upon precept, and even then not as long as we live in this mortal life, for we will have to go even beyond the grave before we reach that perfection. . . . But here we lay the foundation. . . . It is our duty to be better today than we were yesterday, and better tomorrow than we are today."[56]

C. S. Lewis believed this ideal was possible: "The command Be ye perfect is not idealistic gas. Nor is it a command to do the impossible. He is going to make us into creatures that can obey that command. . . . The process will be long and in parts very painful, but that is what we are in for. Nothing less. He meant what He said."[57]

Because of our potential for eternal glory, this mortal probation is more valuable than any earthly acquisition or honor. This is our chance to show our Father and His Son that we care more about Them than about anything the world has to offer. This is our chance to prove that we do not seek first the things of this world but to "build up the kingdom of God, and to establish his righteousness."[58] This is our chance to prove that we understand there *are* such things as right and wrong, good and evil, and these distinctions are established by God, not by man. Truth is *not* relative. Right and wrong cannot be gauged by a sliding scale, nor can they be dictated by popularity, polls, scientific studies, or the approval of the masses.

This is the time to come to understand for ourselves that we know who we are and who we've always been, that we understand why we're here, and that we comprehend who we may ultimately become.

It is as Elder M. Russell Ballard declared: "My dear sisters, we believe in you. We believe in and are counting on your goodness and your strength, your propensity for virtue and valor, your kindness and courage, your strength and resilience. We believe in your mission as women of God. We realize that you are the emotional (and sometimes spiritual) glue that holds families and often ward families together. We believe that the Church simply will not accomplish what it must without your faith and faithfulness, your innate tendency to put the well-being of others ahead of your own, and your spiritual strength and tenacity. And we believe that God's plan is for you to become queens and to receive the highest blessings . . . in time or eternity."[59]

This is the time to come to understand for ourselves that we know who we are and who we've always been, that we understand why we're here, and that we comprehend who we may ultimately become.

The first step in understanding how God sees His daughters—and the first step in coming to understand the privileges women have in God's kingdom—is understanding who we are, who we have always been, and who we may ultimately become.

Chapter 3

GOD EXPECTS WOMEN
TO RECEIVE REVELATION

I have a friend whose devoted service and leadership have blessed
the Saints wherever she has been called to labor. She recently told me
about an unexpected conversation she had with a seasoned priesthood
leader who approached her after she had served for a time in a particular
leadership capacity. She was caught off guard when he said, "I owe you
an apology." Because of this man's breadth of priesthood leadership experience, her surprise at his statement escalated to astonishment when
he admitted, "I didn't know that a woman could receive revelation. But I
can see that you have been receiving revelation for your calling. I am sorry
that I misjudged you and other women as well."

How a man of his experience could have served in so many priesthood leadership capacities without witnessing women receiving revelation—or perhaps even more troublesome, without *expecting* them to
seek direction from heaven—is dumbfounding. But, unfortunately, this
leader is likely not alone in the mistaken assumption that if there is "heavy
lifting" to be done spiritually, women are of little, if any, value.

This priesthood leader's poverty of understanding is in stark contrast to the experience of a young bishop who quickly came to realize that, although the Lord often blessed him with revelation for his ward, it was just as important for him to recognize when other ward leaders were receiving revelation—and to encourage them to actively seek it. He began to learn this principle not long after setting apart a Beehive class president. He was conducting a bishop's youth council when an item arose that concerned Beehive-age girls in particular. In a moment of being tutored by the Spirit, he looked at the Beehive class president and said, "If the Lord has revelation to give us for the Beehive girls in our ward, who do you think He is most likely to send that revelation to first?"

She looked puzzled for a moment or two before answering, with surprise on her face, "Me?"

"Yes," her bishop said, smiling as he taught her and the youth leaders in the room. "If you will ask the Lord what the girls in your class need, He will tell you. It is our job to listen to you."

God expects women to receive revelation. And He expects it of women of all ages. President Henry B. Eyring recounted an experience he and his wife had as they contemplated leaving Ricks College, where he was serving as president, to accept a job with a prestigious corporation. "My wife," President Eyring said, "had a strong impression that we were not to leave Ricks College. I said, 'That's good enough for me.' But she insisted, wisely, that I must get my own revelation. And so I prayed again. This time I did receive direction, in the form of a voice in my mind that said, 'I'll *let* you stay at Ricks College a little longer.'"[1] In President Eyring's own telling

I declare without reservation that our Father will reveal His mind and will to His daughters. Not only that: He expects His daughters to learn how to receive instructions from Him and then seek to do so.

of the story, it was Sister Eyring who first received revelation about the direction they should take.

I had the privilege of serving as a stake Relief Society president under the direction of a stake president who *expected* me to receive revelation. In preparation for one stake conference, he called me to his office and extended the invitation to speak in the Sunday morning session. He outlined the theme of the conference and then asked me to pray and ponder about what the Lord would have me say. Several times between that meeting and the conference, I asked him if there weren't something specific he wanted me to address. Each time, my stake president stated simply, "Sheri, the Lord will tell *you* what He wants you to teach the members of our stake. Whatever He tells you to teach is what I want you to teach." No matter how many times I probed for something more specific, he gave me the same response, turning me to the Lord for my answer. In doing so, he communicated not only that he had faith in me but that the Lord did as well.

My purpose in this chapter is to declare without reservation that our Father will reveal His mind and will to His daughters. Not only that: He *expects* His daughters to learn how to receive instructions from Him and then seek to do so.

IT IS MORE BLESSED TO RECEIVE

We have all heard that "it is more blessed to give than to receive,"[2] and there is no shortage of examples proving this point. One favorite is the account of the faithful widow who cast her meager offering—just two mites—into the treasury. The Savior taught the value of the widow's offering when He said that "this poor widow hath cast more in, than all they which have cast into the treasury: For all they did cast in of their abundance; but she of her want did cast in all that she had, even all her living."[3]

That widow has become an example, an inspiration for all of us to take stock of what we give to the Lord and to others—in material abundance as well as our talents, time, energy, and our hearts. Members of The Church of Jesus Christ of Latter-day Saints believe in giving.

But it is just as crucial that we learn to receive. In fact, our eternal lives depend on it.

God expects women to receive revelation, with emphasis on the word *receive.* Three examples:

1. When twins "struggled together within" Rebekah, she inquired of the Lord rather than asking her prophet-husband Isaac to do so, and she received a revelation about the sons in her womb that would change the destiny of nations.[4]

2. At the fifth meeting of the Relief Society in this dispensation, on April 19, 1842, the women enjoyed an outpouring of the Spirit such that Eliza R. Snow recorded that "nearly all present arose & spoke, and the spirit of the Lord like a purifying stream, refreshed every heart."[5]

3. On a later occasion, when serving as Relief Society general president, Eliza taught the sisters that the Holy Ghost "satisfies and fills up every longing of the human heart, and fills up every vacuum. When I am filled with that Spirit," she continued, "my soul is satisfied, and I can say in good earnest, that the trifling things of the day do not seem to stand in my way at all. But just let me lose my hold of that spirit and power of the Gospel, and partake of the spirit of the world, in the slightest degree, and trouble comes; there is something wrong. I am tried, and what will comfort me? You cannot impart comfort to me that will satisfy the immortal mind, but that which comes from the Fountain above. And is it not our privilege to so live that we can have this constantly flowing into our souls?"[6]

Our Father and His Son want to bless us, teach us, guide us, and talk

Members of The Church of Jesus Christ of Latter-day Saints believe in giving. But it is just as crucial that we learn to receive. In fact, our eternal lives depend on it. God expects women to receive revelation, with emphasis on the word receive.

to us. But we have to learn *how*. If there is a communication gap, the gap is on our side of the conversation.

I'll never forget a question that a friend, a lifelong member of the Church, posed one day. This woman has been a stalwart member her entire life, taught the gospel in countless settings, and served with her husband on several missions to other lands. And yet one evening, she asked in all sincerity, "Is it okay for me to ask the Lord for revelation and for spiritual gifts?" Her question caught me by surprise, so I asked if she would explain what had motivated her statement. "I just wonder if I should bother the Lord with my requests," she replied. As we talked, it became clear that what she was really asking was, "I know that the Lord has time to talk to the prophet and other leaders regarding big issues that affect the Church, but is it right for me to trouble Him with my personal concerns?"

The Lord has answered this question again and again, promising to give unto us "line upon line, precept upon precept, here a little and there a little," making it clear that those who listen have an advantage over those who don't: "Blessed are those who hearken unto my precepts, and lend an ear unto my counsel, for they shall learn wisdom; for *unto him that receiveth I will give more*."[7]

Those who believe they have no need of revelation are increasingly left to themselves, and regardless of how bright, educated or accomplished they are, eventually the adversary will outwit, outfox, and outmaneuver them. It's a given.

What a joy it is, then, to know that, as Elder Bruce R. McConkie explained, "there is no limit to the revelations each member of the Church may receive. It is within the power of every person who has received the gift of the Holy Ghost to see visions, entertain angels, learn the deep and hidden mysteries of the kingdom, and even see the face of God."[8]

There is no quota on prayers, no ceiling on the number of revelations we may receive, no limit on how much we may learn from above, no expiration date or maximum number of punches on our prayer or spiritual gift cards. Moroni taught that "by the power of the Holy Ghost [we] may know the truth of *all things*."[9] The only limitations on our communication with our Heavenly Father are those we impose ourselves. We impose those limitations by *not* seeking, *not* asking, and *not* learning how to receive answers, gifts, and information.

There is no question about what our Father and His Son have promised us. They have promised to tell us, show us, and share everything with us. The only question is about what we are willing to receive, because receiving requires action on our part. Elder Richard G. Scott explained that "the Lord will not force you to learn. You must exercise your agency to *authorize* the Spirit to teach you. As you make this a practice in your life you will be more perceptive to the feelings that come with spiritual guidance. Then, when that guidance comes, sometimes when you least expect it, you will recognize it more clearly."[10]

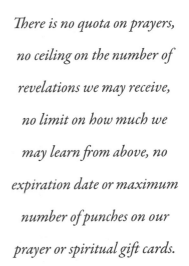

There is no quota on prayers, no ceiling on the number of revelations we may receive, no limit on how much we may learn from above, no expiration date or maximum number of punches on our prayer or spiritual gift cards.

We authorize the Spirit to teach us when we study, seek, attend meetings with an open heart, pray, ponder, worship in the temple, serve, and ask questions of the Lord. With the rarest of exceptions, we have to *do something* in order to receive blessings, gain knowledge, and receive revelation. Knowledge from heaven doesn't just fall from the sky.

During the time I served in the Relief Society general presidency, the Church instituted a new security system that required Church employees, general officers, and others who frequented the extended Church campus in downtown Salt Lake City—meaning Temple Square and the blocks housing the Conference Center, Church Office Building, Joseph Smith Memorial Building, Relief Society Building, and Church Administration Building—to wear identification badges. Because our presidency had served nearly five years when the new system went into operation and we were easily recognized around Church headquarters, we rarely had much cause to use our new ID badges. So I didn't develop the habit of wearing mine, though I usually carried it with me.

In the Saturday session of the April 2002 general conference, our presidency was released. We came and went to the sessions of conference in the manner typical for General Authorities and general officers of the Church—through a series of tunnels that connect the various buildings on the Church campus.

I had been assigned to speak the next day, on Sunday morning, at an early-morning devotional for all Church hosts and hostesses serving in the Conference Center, Tabernacle, and other Church campus buildings. I was to be at the Little Theater in the Conference Center at six o'clock on the Sunday morning of general conference. As I drove to the Conference Center that morning, it dawned on me that heavy double doors located at certain points along the tunnel might not be open that early.

Sure enough, the very first door in the tunnel was still locked. Wondering what to do, I noticed a buzzer and intercom. I pushed the buzzer to alert a Church security officer, identified who I was, explained my assignment in the Little Theater, and asked if he would let me through the door. "Sister Dew, do you have your ID badge with you?" he asked. When I rummaged through my binder and found it, the officer responded, "Your badge gives you access to all of these doors. Didn't you know that?"

"You mean, all this time I've been carrying with me a badge that would give me entrance to all of these underground tunnels on the Church campus, and I didn't even know it?"

"Yes," he said, and then, quickly bringing me down to earth, added, "and because you were released yesterday morning, enjoy the badge for the remainder of today, because tomorrow it will be deactivated."

As promised, all of the doors through the tunnel sprang open as I held my badge in front of the sensor located next to each of them. And, also as predicted, the next day the card no longer worked. The privilege was gone.

The irony was unmistakable. For months I had carried with me a badge that had given me privileges I hadn't understood or taken advantage of. I had not understood that badge's power.

THE GIFT AND POWER OF THE HOLY GHOST

As baptized, confirmed members of the Church, we carry the "gift and the power of the Holy Ghost"[11] with us. We have access to truth, knowledge, godly power, revelation, peace (even when circumstances are not peaceful), and the constant companionship of the third member of the Godhead. Membership in The Church of Jesus Christ of Latter-day Saints comes with profound spiritual privileges. But they are privileges we must exercise our agency to learn about and use, or they lie dormant.

Nephi attempted to teach his people about the gift of the Holy Ghost—that the Holy Ghost had the capacity to teach them *all things* that they should do, and that they could speak with the tongue of angels.[12] But he was ultimately constrained: "The Spirit stoppeth mine utterance," he explained, "and I am left to mourn because of the unbelief, and the wickedness, and the ignorance, and the stiffneckedness of men; *for they will not search knowledge, nor understand great knowledge,* when it is given unto them in plainness, even as plain as word can be."[13]

Membership in The Church of Jesus Christ of Latter-day Saints comes with profound spiritual privileges. But they are privileges we must exercise our agency to learn about and use, or they lie dormant.

Elder Heber C. Kimball said Joseph Smith experienced the same kind of frustration: "The greatest torment [the Prophet Joseph] had and the greatest mental suffering was because this people would not live up to their privileges. . . . He said sometimes that he felt . . . as though he were pent up in an acorn shell, and all because the people . . . *would not prepare themselves to receive the rich treasures of wisdom and knowledge that he had to impart.* He could have revealed a great many things to us if we had been ready; but he said there were many things that we could not receive because we lacked that diligence . . . necessary to entitle us to those choice things of the kingdom."[14]

The Lord will not force His privileges, power, or knowledge on anyone. On the other hand, Joseph Smith taught that "the Holy Ghost is a revelator," and "no man can receive the Holy Ghost without receiving revelation."[16] He also explained how inclusive our Father and His Son are when it comes to personal revelation: "God hath not revealed anything to Joseph, but what He will make known unto the Twelve, and even the least Saint may know all things as fast as he is able to bear them, for the day must come when no man need say to his neighbor, Know ye the Lord; for all shall know Him (who remain) from the least to the greatest."[17]

We are in large measure the ones who determine what we will receive in mortality and through all eternity.

Imagine! You and I have the potential of receiving what Joseph Smith received. This is the man who communed with the Father and the Son, who opened the dispensation of the fulness of times, who was taught and mentored by angels and ancient prophets. This is the prophet who received a revelation promising us wisdom that would reach to heaven, an understanding of all the mysteries of the Lord's kingdom and the wonders of eternity.[18] The prophet who received a revelation while incarcerated in Liberty Jail promising that God would give us knowledge "by his Holy Spirit, yea, by the unspeakable gift of the Holy Ghost, that has not been revealed since the world was until now," which revelation went on to include a sweeping promise: "As well might man stretch forth his puny arm to stop the Missouri river in its decreed course, or to turn it up stream, as to hinder the Almighty from pouring down knowledge from heaven upon the heads of the Latter-day Saints."[19]

We are in large measure the ones who determine what we will receive in mortality and through all eternity.

No one wants us to talk to our Father, receive counsel from Him, and learn how His kingdom operates more than He does. *"Whosoever will come may come* and partake of the waters of life freely,"* Alma taught, "and whosoever will not come the same is not compelled to come."[20]

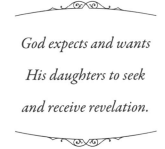

God expects and wants His daughters to seek and receive revelation.

If we want to receive revelation and are willing to learn how, we'll receive revelation. There is perhaps no more frequent invitation or reassuring promise in all of scripture than, "Seek me diligently and ye shall find me; ask, and ye shall receive; knock, and it shall be opened unto you."[21] This invitation contains a promise that can literally change our lives. "If thou shalt ask, thou shalt receive revelation upon revelation, knowledge upon knowledge, that thou mayest know the mysteries and peaceable things— that which bringeth joy, that which bringeth life eternal."[22] This is the ultimate access to a Friend in high places.

God expects and wants His daughters to seek and receive revelation.

We have access to information from heaven that no other people in the history of the world have had. Because His own people weren't ready or worthy, there were things the Savior could not teach them during His mortal ministry. There were things the Jews didn't know. There were things the Nephites didn't know. But in our day, the dispensation during which "nothing shall be withheld,"[23] all knowledge, power, and privileges have been restored.

Since that spring day when the young Joseph Smith walked into a grove of trees to ask which Church was true, we have known that the heavens are open. Said President Spencer W. Kimball: "Someone has said that we live in a day in which God, if there be a God, chooses to be silent, but The Church of Jesus Christ of Latter-day Saints proclaims to the world that neither the Father nor the Son is silent. They are vocal and . . . constantly express a willingness, indeed an eagerness, to maintain communication with men."[24]

Our challenge is one of vision and desire—the vision to know what is possible, and the desire to seek to learn the language of revelation.

THE LANGUAGE OF REVELATION

Elder Bruce R. McConkie put the importance of learning the language of revelation in context: "Education and intellectuality are devoutly to be desired. But when contrasted with spiritual endowments, they are of but slight and passing worth. From an eternal perspective, what each of us needs is a Ph.D. in faith and righteousness. The things that will profit us everlastingly are not the power to reason, but the ability to receive revelation."[25]

How do we learn to access the gift and power of the Holy Ghost? In other words, how do we learn the language of revelation?

There is no step-by-step formula to communicating with heaven, but there are certain keys that help us learn this language and provide an atmosphere where the Spirit will dwell and minister. Faith in the Lord Jesus Christ is foundational. Obedience, purity, and immersion in the scriptures are also essential.

In my early twenties, after praying and fasting and struggling to make an important life decision, I sought a priesthood blessing from a trusted friend and mentor. During a conversation before the blessing, my friend asked what the Lord had already told me. I confessed that I couldn't tell, that I could feel the presence of the Spirit but that I didn't very often feel I was getting information from the Spirit. He then posed a question that literally changed my spiritual life: "Have you asked the Lord to teach you what it feels like when He's communicating with you through the Holy Ghost?"

I had never asked that question, but that night I began to. I did not have some magical experience where suddenly the voice of the Lord became discernible. But interestingly, I began almost immediately to see things in the scriptures that I hadn't seen before—especially how frequently the scriptures include accounts of direct communication between heaven and someone on earth. Over time and with regular study, I noticed there were patterns involved when God or other heavenly beings talked to mortals on earth. And it seemed as though those patterns and examples were everywhere.

The scriptures are *the* handbook for learning the language of revelation. They teach the Lord's vocabulary and language, the circumstances that both invite and alienate the Spirit, and the manner in which the Lord interacts with mankind. They are also a conduit for revelation. Regular immersion in holy writ pays dividends. Studying the scriptures is a key to learning the difference between *feeling* the Spirit and *hearing the voice* of the Spirit. The Book of Mormon, in particular, can act as a kind of Urim and Thummim in helping us understand the things of God.

Elder Richard G. Scott explained how the scriptures aid revelation: "When I am faced with a very difficult matter, . . . I fast. I pray to find and understand scriptures that will be helpful. That process is cyclical. I start reading a passage of scripture; I ponder what the verse means and pray for inspiration. I then ponder and pray to know if I have captured all the Lord wants me to do. Often more impressions come with increased understanding of doctrine. I have found that pattern to be a good way to learn from the scriptures."[26]

The scriptures are a foundational key to learning the language of revelation.

Another key is purity. Whereas impurity drives the Spirit away, purity invites the Spirit. Anything—movies, language, websites, apps, music, artwork, books, downloads, clothing, thoughts, feelings, actions, you

> *The scriptures are the handbook for learning the language of revelation. They teach the Lord's vocabulary and language, the circumstances that both invite and alienate the Spirit, and the manner in which the Lord interacts with mankind.*

name it—that is coarse, angry, profane, resentful, vulgar, dishonest, hard-hearted, immodest, or immoral, or that in any way supports the adversary's agenda, will drive the Spirit away or prevent the Spirit from coming.

It is not that the Spirit can't come, it is that He won't.

Alternatively, a pure and forgiving heart, modesty, expressions of love, kindness, gentility, and declarations of faith invite the Spirit.

During one general conference I had an unforgettable experience. I had fasted and prayed in preparation and had identified a question I hoped the Lord would answer during the conference. In the first session, during an address by a member of the Quorum of the Twelve Apostles, I had a distinct impression that had absolutely nothing to do with the question I had on my mind. The impression was simply, "Sheri, you have the TV on too much."

My initial reaction was, I'm sorry to say, a bit defensive. "Surely I don't have the TV on that much," I thought to myself. But as the conference progressed, and as I humbled myself, I realized that I had it on more than I had thought—often as "background noise," but on nonetheless. I charted a new course and started listening to general conference addresses as I got ready in the morning and drifted to sleep at night. Over time, I could discern that the feeling in my home—not to mention the attitude I took with me through the day—softened.

Recently, I had the impression that it was time to turn off the TV even more. That led to further action and more restraints. My media consumption has always been tame, but these repeated impressions are helping me free my home from the influence of the adversary. It is about walking away from the world. Admittedly, this takes vigilance, and I am far from perfect at it. But as President Spencer W. Kimball taught, "The cultivation of Christlike qualities is a demanding and relentless task—it is not for the seasonal worker or for those who will not stretch themselves, again and again."[27]

Increased purity takes effort. But purity is a key to inviting the presence of the Holy Ghost and the ministering of angels.

We live in a world that flaunts filth. The gaudier and more perverse, the better. Everything from network TV to social media sites encourages pithy and clever though vulgar language and behavior. It takes real work to keep our environment, minds, hearts, thoughts, and bodies pure. As we exercise our agency and engage in that work, we *authorize* the Holy Ghost to help us and teach us how to accomplish it. And there is power in purity, for "the Spirit of the Lord doth not dwell in unholy temples."[28]

Parley P. Pratt taught how tangible the impact of the Holy Ghost is on those who seek to have the Spirit with them: "The gift of the Holy Ghost adapts itself to all . . . organs and attributes. It quickens all the intellectual faculties, increases, enlarges, expands, and purifies all natural passions and affections and adapts them, by the gift of wisdom, to their lawful use. It inspires, develops, cultivates, and matures all the fine-toned sympathies, joys, tastes, kindred feelings, and affections of our nature. It inspires virtue, kindness, goodness, tenderness, gentleness, and charity. It develops beauty of person, form, and features. It tends to health, vigor, animation, and social feeling. It invigorates all the faculties of the physical and intellectual man. It strengthens and gives tonic and tone to the nerves. In short, it is, as it were, marrow to the bone, joy to the heart, light to the eyes, music to the ears, and life to the whole being."[29]

Increased purity takes effort. But purity is a key to inviting the presence of the Holy Ghost and the ministering of angels.

When the Holy Ghost is operating with us, we're smarter, wiser, kinder and more filled with charity, the pure love of Christ. And we actually look more like our true selves as well.

When all is said and done, a primary pursuit for those desiring to excel at the language of revelation is to make their spiritual life the dominating characteristic of who they are. Elder Russell M. Nelson explained that "danger lurks when we divide ourselves with expressions such as 'my private life,' 'my professional life,' or even 'my best behavior.' Living life in separate compartments can lead to internal conflict and exhausting tension. To escape that tension, many people unwisely resort to addicting substances, pleasure seeking, or self-indulgence, which in turn produce more tension, thus creating a vicious cycle. Inner peace comes only as we maintain the integrity of truth in all aspects of our lives. When we covenant to follow the Lord and obey His commandments, we accept His standards in every thought, action, and deed."[30]

> *A primary pursuit for those desiring to excel at the language of revelation is to make their spiritual life the dominating characteristic of who they are.*

The natural man and woman *are* enemies to God. Men and women who yield "to the enticings of the Holy Spirit"[31] are those positioned to learn the language of revelation.

THE BLESSINGS OF REVELATION

The Prophet Joseph taught that "a person may profit by noticing the first intimation of the spirit of revelation; for instance, when you feel pure intelligence flowing into you, it may give you sudden strokes of ideas, so that by noticing it, you may find it fulfilled the same day or soon; (i.e.) Those things that were presented unto your minds by the Spirit of God, will come to pass; and thus by learning the Spirit of God and understanding it, you may grow into the principle of revelation."[32]

To receive revelation we haven't yet received, we will likely need to seek in ways we haven't sought before and do things we haven't done.

If you haven't read the Book of Mormon lately, start now. Experiment upon the word.[33] Read the entire book in a short time to remind yourself of major themes. Then start again, looking for patterns and connections and points of doctrine that prophets emphasize again and again. If you've never studied the four New Testament Gospels alongside Third Nephi, try that—you'll enjoy the process. It is a wonderful way to study what the Savior repeatedly taught during His mortal ministry in the Holy Land and His postmortal ministry to those on the American continent. It is difficult to experiment on the word if we don't know the word.

If you aren't sure what the Savior did for you through His infinite Atonement, look for every passage of scripture you can find where He declares His divinity and explains what He did for us—including that He made it possible for our broken hearts and wounds to be healed, that He will "succor" or run to us in times of need, that He will heal us from sin when we repent, that He will and can help turn our weakness into strength.[34] Seek to understand why Nephi prophesied that the Savior would "rise from the dead, with healing in his wings."[35] We need to think about Him more.

Our Father and His Son desire to shower gifts upon us, but we must ask.

If you haven't been to the temple lately or haven't established a pattern of regular temple worship (assuming there is a temple within a reasonable distance), just go! Establish that regular pattern. Allow time while there to ponder and pray. Ask to understand more about the endowment you have received. Ask to understand the depth and breadth of the sealing covenant. Ask how to banish Satan. Ask God to help you learn how to part the veil that separates us from Him and His Son.

If you've never been able to get a sense about how Heavenly Father feels about you, read Doctrine and Covenants 138 and Abraham 3, paying particular attention to verses about the "noble and great" ones. Ask Heavenly Father to help you understand more about your life's mission.

If you're not sure which spiritual gifts you've been given, or how to ask and qualify for additional gifts, or why we're encouraged to "covet earnestly the best gifts,"[36] study 1 Corinthians 12–14, Moroni 10, and Doctrine and Covenants 46, and ask the Lord to tutor you as you read and ponder. Our Father and His Son desire to shower gifts upon us, but we must ask.

If you have a temper or lack confidence in yourself, what spiritual gifts might you seek to counterbalance those areas of weakness? If you feel unsure about the direction of your life or are struggling with your testimony or have an addiction, what spiritual gifts would help you?

President George Q. Cannon encouraged us to pray for gifts of the Spirit that would countermand and eradicate our weaknesses: "If any of us are imperfect, it is our duty to pray for the gift that will make us perfect. Have I imperfections? I am full of them. What is my duty? To pray to God to give me the gifts that will correct these imperfections. If I am an angry man, it is my duty to pray for charity, which suffereth long and is kind. Am I an envious man? It is my duty to seek for charity, which envieth not. So with all the gifts of the Gospel. They are intended for this purpose."[37]

Spiritual gifts are given to those who seek after them, and they are given to those whom the Lord can trust to use them to bless others.

Spiritual gifts are given to those who seek after them, and they are given to those whom the Lord can trust to use them to bless others.

If some of the prevailing social winds run counter to gospel doctrine, and that conflict concerns or confuses you, search the scriptures and the teachings of living prophets, seers, and revelators, and seek to understand the Lord's way and to recognize how and why the Lord's way differs from man's. As you study, pray for the gifts of wisdom and discernment.

If you're not sure if you're feeling the presence of the Holy Ghost, or you wonder if you are accurately translating the impressions you're receiving, ask the Lord to tutor you through the ministering of the Spirit. Ask Him to lead you to scriptures and to teachings of living prophets that will help you grow in the spirit of revelation. Look for every evidence in the scriptures of direct communication between heaven and mortals on earth, because in those accounts lie instructions for learning the language of revelation.

If you think you don't have enough time for any of this, consider cutting back on the time you're plugged in—to blogs, websites, iPads, smart phones, and social media. We live in a wired world, and technology provides fantastic advantages. But Facebook, Pinterest, and Instagram don't have the power to exalt anyone. Unplug from the world long enough to allow the Spirit to take over.

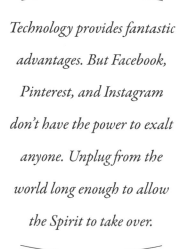

Technology provides fantastic advantages. But Facebook, Pinterest, and Instagram don't have the power to exalt anyone. Unplug from the world long enough to allow the Spirit to take over.

It is difficult to hear the whisperings of the Spirit with headphones or earbuds on. Even a few minutes of gospel study a day, over an extended period of time, will pay important spiritual dividends. You'll be astounded at the impact regular immersion in the gospel has on your ability to feel and hear the Spirit.

THE SPIRIT SPEAKS OF THINGS AS THEY REALLY ARE

Several years ago, the winter in my neighborhood was long and harsh. Because I live on the side of a mountain, deer wandered into my yard all winter long scavenging for food. They wrecked everything! Once spring came, I faced the challenge of repairing months' worth of damage from those cute but obnoxious Bambis.

For several weeks, I spent every evening I could spare pulling out damaged perennials and planting dozens of new shrubs and flowers. It was a lot of work.

One evening I finally finished, swept the dirt off the sidewalk, and went to bed. Early the next morning, as I glanced out a front window, I noticed dirt on the sidewalk. Knowing I had swept everything carefully the night before, I stepped outside for a closer look and was shocked with what I saw. Dozens of plants were gone—simply gone. This time deer were not the culprits. The plants had vanished, leaving holes all over the yard.

Not knowing quite what to do about stolen plants, I finally called the police to see if they had had reports of other damaged yards in the area. They sent a policeman, who handed me a complaint report to fill out and began walking around the neighborhood. As I worked my way through the questions, I momentarily lost track of the officer. Suddenly he reappeared and announced, "I found your plants," and he motioned me to follow him. We walked around to the backyard of my newly moved-in neighbors, where a number of mangled flowers were lined up on the patio. "I assume these are your plants," he said. When I nodded yes, he knocked on the front door.

What a way to meet the neighbors, I thought, as horrified parents quickly put two and two together and realized what had happened. Moments later they came marching out with the cutest little six-year-old girl you've ever seen. Then it was I who was horrified: *Oh, no,* I thought, *I've called the police on a six-year-old!*

This little girl and her young friends had apparently been drawn to my yard by the new flowers. When they gently tugged on the flowers—which hadn't yet taken root—they came up easily. One thing led to another, and in short order the little girl and her gang of flower-snatchers had done their work.

With the mystery of the missing perennials solved, we all made amends, I bought new plants to replace those whose roots had been damaged in the escapade, and I set out to replant the yard. But as I did so, I couldn't help but think about lessons that episode taught.

The first lesson is an obvious one: Are we rooted? The only reason those plants came up so easily was that they hadn't had time to take root. Are we rooted in the Lord and His gospel? If we aren't, the adversary will at some point uproot us with his equivalent of a six-year-old—meaning, it won't take much.

The second message seemed equally compelling. The flower is what attracted the little girl, but it is the root of the plant that gives it life and makes it grow. When the root dies, the flower cannot bloom. The homely root buried in the ground is actually more important than the showy flower on top.

Today we are in danger of being consumed with appearances. But it is what's inside of us that makes us grow and develop and live. Since that episode with the missing plants, I have often asked myself, What does the part of me that I *can't see* look like? What do my courage, virtue, and integrity look like? What does my heart look like? What do my faith and testimony look like? How deep are my spiritual roots?

Because today falsehood is packaged creatively and persuasively, there is no skill more important to our eternal well-being than learning the language of revelation.

Some things are more important than others. And though we all want to look as appealing as we can, appearance is rarely the most important thing. The part we can't see is almost always more important than the parts we can.

Our spiritual lives, our knowledge and understanding of the gospel, our ability to receive revelation are simply far more important than so much of what we spend our time attending to.

But becoming rooted spiritually takes effort on our part. Because today falsehood is packaged creatively and persuasively, there is no skill more important to our eternal well-being than learning the language of revelation. The world is filled with "servants of Satan" who "uphold his work."[38] But because "the Spirit speaketh the truth and lieth not,"[39] we can learn to discern what is true and what is not. We can learn to see through even brilliantly packaged falsehoods. Truth in a world filled with half-truths carefully disguised and persuasively marketed is worth more than its weight in gold. For truth is a "knowledge of things as they are, and as they were, and as they are to come."[40]

WOMEN ARE RECEPTIVE TO THE SPIRIT

The accounts of righteous women receiving revelation in this dispensation are nearly endless. Women seeking direction can and will be guided from on high. That guidance will come in many forms. "One of the most memorable and powerful patterns of communication by the Spirit is through dreams,"[41] taught Elder Richard G. Scott.

One devoted mother living in Alberta, Canada, shared the following account of a dream that inspired her about how to help her son:

My husband was the bishop of our large ward with over a hundred youth. He was also a busy doctor who not only had his own practice but was also on faculty at a nearby university. We had six active children ranging from ages 17 to 5. It seemed that I was going it alone much of the time.

The hope and prayer of any caring Latter-day Saint woman is that her children will choose good friends. Even with a large youth group, and though our eldest son always went to seminary and church, he connected more with friends outside the Church. These friends came to our home often, and we liked them. They were decent, polite young men. But it was during this time that I had a powerful dream.

I found myself in the midst of a crowded boxing arena. I had never attended a boxing match before. I had only watched the sport in the movies and there was the same fighting spirit and energy in the building as I'd seen on the big screen.

After settling in I rose with the crowd as they stood up to cheer. I looked down at the ring and to my horror discovered that my son and one of his closest friends were the contestants. My heart sank. "What on earth is he doing here?" I thought. The friend was throwing hard punches to my son's head. With each hit, his head was abruptly forced to the right, then to the left, then back again—just like the pounding punches a professional boxer would throw. One time when my son's head was hit in my direction, he looked up at me with a smile on his face and said, "This is fun." Over and over again the assault continued. My son just stood there with his hands at each side. Why would he walk into a fight willingly, enjoy the battle, and not protect himself?

"Get out of the ring!" I yelled again, and again. But he wouldn't hear me and the fight continued with my son looking like a happy, limp rag doll. Calling him by name I desperately screamed again, "Fight back! Do something!" But he would not hear.

In despair, I sank into my seat feeling helpless and hopeless as the crowd cheered on. Mothers are to protect their children, but I couldn't do a thing. His life seemed out of my reach and influence.

Then the thought came that I should sing a song. Willing to try anything, I began to quietly sing a gentle melody very much out of place in that dreadful setting. Though the music rang through the air, the audience seemed oblivious. I had not been singing long when I saw my beaten son straighten up, look around, shake his head as if coming to his senses, and turn his head in the direction of the music. He walked away from the fight, out of the ring, and toward me and the music.

I pondered this dream for days and came to realize that I was being told that my son was taking a greater beating from his friends than we could see from the outside. I also realized that if music captured his attention during the fight, then music might also be a source of help for him.

After much thought and prayer, it came to me that I should invite some youth over to our house for Sunday-night sing-alongs. There were three young men in our ward whom I knew had musical ability. The invitation was extended, and they willingly came.

Though they at first struggled to sing in harmony with each other, in time their abilities and confidence increased as did my love for them. They eventually performed widely. More important, this regular activity at our home had a marked impact on our son. It is something I would have never conceived were it not for that dream and then praying to understand the dream.[42]

This prayerful mother learned many things through the revelatory process: that through service and sacrifice, love increases; that we can't always see the incredible pressure teenagers are under; that when a child wanders he is more likely to respond to words of love and encouragement than to scolding; that there is power in good music; and that the Lord hears and answers prayers, even sending dreams and revelation to interpret the dream to a mother who is seeking.

A CENTRAL THEME OF THE RESTORATION

If there is a central theme of the Restoration, surely it is that the heavens are open to us, the Lord wants to speak to us, and heavenly messengers watch over and teach those who seek their help.

Our Father knows what He needs us to do. He is entirely familiar with each of our divine errands. He has made it possible for us to receive direction from Him through the ministering and instrumentality of the Holy Ghost.

President Henry B. Eyring has taught: "Your life is carefully watched over, as was mine. The Lord knows both what He will need you to do and what you will need to know. He is kind and He is all-knowing. So, you can with confidence expect that He has prepared opportunities for you to learn in preparation for the service you will give. You will not recognize those opportunities perfectly, as I did not. But when you put the spiritual things first in your life, you will be blessed to feel directed toward certain learning and you will be motivated to work harder. You will recognize later that your power to serve was increased, and you will be grateful."[43]

Our Father knows what He needs us to do. He is entirely familiar with each of our divine errands. He has made it possible for us to receive direction from Him through the ministering and instrumentality of the Holy Ghost. Communing with Him is a sacred privilege.

He expects His daughters to both seek and receive revelation. Cultivating the ability to do so is crucial to gaining a full understanding, under the direction of the Spirit, of who we are as daughters of God.

Chapter 4

GOD IS PERFECT AND SO IS HIS SON

During a holiday party years ago, a friend responsible for the "entertainment" brought a 2000-piece jigsaw puzzle for us to put together in a lightning round. The challenge was not only the speed with which we were to assemble the large puzzle but the fact that the pieces came in a plastic grocery bag with no picture of the completed puzzle and with miscellaneous pieces from other random puzzles mixed in. And to make it just a little more "fun," key pieces from the main puzzle were missing.

What a dumb game! It wasn't fun at all for me, and I was relieved when the lightning round expired. The whole thing seemed pointless. Without a clear picture of what the puzzle would look like, the exercise was harder than it needed to be if not nearly impossible to complete.

The analogy is simple: Without a clear picture of why we are here, life could seem pointless, or at least purposeless. But in reality, life is anything but pointless. Mortality is a vital step toward immortality.

A FRAMEWORK

We accept as doctrine the following key truths, which truths paint a picture of who we are, why we are here, and who we may ultimately become:

- We lived premortally, and gender is eternal.[1]

- Our Heavenly Father created both men and women, who are His beloved spirit sons and daughters.

- The only mission of the Father and the Son, Their work and Their glory, is to "bring to pass the immortality and eternal life of man."[2] In other words, it is to give each of us the best conceivable chance to ultimately live where They live and become as They are.

- In order to accomplish this, our Father created a plan designed to help His children achieve their ultimate potential of becoming like He is. We sometimes refer to this as the plan of salvation. Another name is the plan of happiness.

- The Father and the Son created the earth[3] to provide a place where we would be separated from Their presence, experience true moral agency, and face the consequences of our decisions.

- Our Father's plan called for man to fall. Elder Orson F. Whitney described the Fall as having "a twofold direction— downward, yet forward. It brought man into the world and set his feet upon progression's highway."[4]

- Because man would fall, we would need a Savior to work an infinite Atonement and to redeem those who would choose to repent and seek to overcome the natural man. The Father chose and sent His most valiant Child, His Firstborn, His Only Begotten Son, to be our Savior.

- In order for our Father's spirit sons and daughters to progress, it would be imperative for them to leave premortality through birth into mortality, receive physical bodies, and "gain earthly experience to progress toward perfection." Thus, "marriage between a man and a woman is ordained of God," and "the family is central to the Creator's plan for the eternal destiny of His children."[5] There is nothing more important for a man and woman than to join as husband and wife in the new and everlasting covenant of marriage, keep those covenants, rear children in righteousness, and give their children the best chance to choose the better part.[6]

- The Savior's own Church would need to be restored in the dispensation of the fulness of times so that His power, His authority, and His ordinances could be available to those who gained a witness of its truthfulness and qualified for His blessings.

- Because living in a telestial environment, separated from our heavenly parents, would be fraught with moral and spiritual danger, we would need access to heavenly power—power much greater than our own. Power would be available to men and women through faith in the Lord Jesus Christ and His Atonement, through the gift of the Holy Ghost and the ministering of angels, and it would also be available to men and women alike through the restoration of the priesthood. Both men and women would have full access to this power, though in different ways.

THE RESTORATION OF THE LORD'S CHURCH

Our Father has no higher goal, no greater purpose, than to help us ultimately live where He lives and as He lives. He has promised to help all who choose to follow Him and His Son "progress toward perfection and ultimately realize their divine destiny as heirs of eternal life."[7] This is our Father's plan of happiness for His children.

Our Father's plan called for a Savior to redeem all mankind from their sins. Jesus Christ was born of Mary in the meridian of time, and during His life He established His Church. During His ministry, the Savior taught the same gospel that had been revealed to prophets such as Adam, Noah, Abraham, and Moses. Though difficult to imagine (although it had happened in previous dispensations), many rejected even Jesus Himself.

Following the Savior's death and the deaths of His Apostles, the Lord's Church, along with the Lord's power and authority, was taken from the earth. A restoration of His Church was necessary to return His doctrine, ordinances, power, and authority to the earth. Most Christian theologians and historians have assumed and taught for centuries that Christ's Church survived intact. In fact, LDS scholar Hugh Nibley believed that most theologians have felt their responsibility toward the primitive Church was "to describe it—not question it."[8]

Our Father has no higher goal, no greater purpose, than to help us ultimately live where He lives and as He lives.

Elder Orson F. Whitney told of a Catholic theologian who evaluated the question of the need for a Restoration in this way: "You Mormons are all ignoramuses. You don't even know the strength of your own position. It is so strong that there is only one other tenable in the whole Christian world, and that is the position of the Catholic Church. The issue is between Catholicism and Mormonism. If we are right, you are wrong; if you are right, we are wrong. . . . The Protestants haven't a leg to stand on. For, if we are wrong, they are wrong with us, since they were a part of us and went out from us; while if we are right, they are apostates whom we cut off long ago. If we have the apostolic succession from St. Peter, as we claim, there is no need of Joseph Smith and Mormonism; but if we have not that succession, then such a man as Joseph Smith was necessary, and Mormonism's attitude is the only consistent one. It is either the perpetuation of the gospel from ancient times, or the restoration of the gospel in latter days."[9]

That Restoration commenced in the spring of 1820 when God the Father and His Son Jesus Christ appeared to fourteen-year-old Joseph Smith in a grove of trees in upstate New York. In response to Joseph's question about which church he should join, the Father and the Son told him to join none of them, for the religious "professors" of the day "draw near to me with their lips, but their hearts are far from me, they teach for doctrines the commandments of men, having a form of godliness, but they deny the power thereof."[10]

This Church is not just a nice church filled with nice people doing nice things. It is the Lord's Church, restored to the earth.

In his last general conference address, President Gordon B. Hinckley testified about this unparalleled event: "I affirm my witness of the calling of the Prophet Joseph, of his works, of the sealing of his testimony with his blood as a martyr to the eternal truth. . . . [We] are faced with the stark question of accepting the truth of the First Vision and that which followed it. On the question of its validity lies the very validity of this Church. If it is the truth, and I testify that it is, then the work in which we are engaged is the most important work on the earth."[11]

With this remarkable heavenly manifestation began the process of restoring the gospel to the earth, complete with the Lord's power or priesthood, authority, and all priesthood ordinances necessary for salvation.

Thus, this Church is not just a nice church filled with nice people doing nice things. Nor is it an American church or a nineteenth-century church. It is the Lord's Church, restored to the earth, and is called The Church of Jesus Christ of Latter-day Saints. The Lord Himself told the Nephites: "How be it my church save it be called in my name?"[12] And He also made it clear to the Prophet Joseph, "For thus shall my church be called in the last days, even The Church of Jesus Christ of Latter-day Saints."[13]

This Church is not the Church of Joseph Smith or Brigham Young, though we regard both as prophets. It is not the Church of Gordon B. Hinckley or Thomas S. Monson. It is not even the Church of the Happy Family, though the Church's unrelenting, protective stance about the family is well known.[14] It is The Church of Jesus Christ of Latter-day Saints. Because this Church belongs to the Lord, everything in it belongs to Him as well—the organizational structure, governance, ordinances, covenants, commandments, power, and authority. Everything. It is *all* His.

It is an intriguing fact that from the time of the Apostasy until the early nineteenth century when the gospel was restored, no church was named after Jesus Christ. The reformer Martin Luther seemed to instinctively understand that those following him shouldn't name a church after him: "I pray you leave my name alone and call yourselves not 'Lutherans' but 'Christians,'" he implored. "Who is Luther? My teaching is not mine. I have not been crucified for anyone. . . . How then does it befit me, a miserable bag of dust and ashes, to give my name to the children of Christ? Cease, my dear friends, to cling to these party names and distinctions; away with them all; let us call ourselves only 'Christians' after Him from whom our teaching comes."[15]

About the issue of the Lord's Church being named after Him, Elder James E. Talmage taught: "There are churches named after their place of origin—as the Church of England; other sects are designated in honor of their famous promoters—as Lutherans, Calvinists, Wesleyans; others are known from some peculiarity of creed or doctrine—as Methodists, Presbyterians, and Baptists; but down to the beginning of the nineteenth century there was no church even claiming name or title as the Church of Christ."[16]

The very foundation of The Church of Jesus Christ of Latter-day Saints had beginnings that far predate anything on this earth, as Elder Russell M. Nelson taught: "This Church stands on a unique foundation, anchored to a bedrock of timeless truth. . . . The holy cause in which we are engaged did not begin in 1820 in the state of New York. It did not begin in Bethlehem. It did not begin in the Garden of Eden. The underpinnings of the everlasting gospel were in place even before the world was."[17]

OUR WAYS ARE NOT THE LORD'S WAYS

There is a tendency among some to contrast and compare the practices, beliefs, and governance of the Lord's Church with those of any number of man-made organizations: businesses, charities, governments, universities, and even other religions. Though we have been admonished to trust the Lord with all our hearts and "lean not unto [our] own understanding,"[18] and to not seek to "counsel the Lord, but to take counsel from his hand,"[19] we instinctively tend to evaluate things from our own perspective and based on whatever paradigms we have seen elsewhere.

But any comparison of a secular organization with the Lord's Church will inevitably expose differences. This should be expected. Secular organizations and the Lord's Church will never match. The structure, purpose, and rules of governance won't ever be the same because man-made organizations are led by men, whereas the Church is led by God. Said Wilford Woodruff, "I want to get this principle into your minds, that God Almighty is guiding the course of His Church and Kingdom, not we."[20]

The ways of man are not the ways of the Lord, who said through the prophet Isaiah: "For as the heavens are higher than the earth, so are my ways higher than your ways, and my thoughts than your thoughts."[21] And as Jacob taught, it is impossible to understand all of God's ways except through revelation.[22]

The Lord doesn't do things the way we do them or see things as we see them. Our Father and His Son are Gods. The gap between Deity and mortal man is not only mammoth in distance and scope, it is also incomprehensible to our puny, finite minds. This is why anyone who believes that he or she knows better than the Lord how He should organize His

Church displays a stunning kind of arrogance. How could any of us possibly know better than He how to structure the Church?

Suggesting that the Lord's kingdom should be organized and led like man-made institutions seems particularly odd during an era in which the fallibility of man is constantly on display. It doesn't take much effort to identify governments, businesses, universities, athletic teams, and even humanitarian organizations that are in serious trouble. Scour the *Wall Street Journal* and leading online news sources any day of the week and read all about them. Businesses fail and leave investors holding the bag. Trusted clergymen, leaders, and coaches are implicated in mind-boggling offenses and abuses of power. Politicians become embroiled in their own agendas rather than the best interests of the people they represent and serve. This is not the case with all leaders or all organizations, of course. But flaws abound in the day-to-day workings of ordinary mortals. Men and women do the best they can. But nothing we create compares with what the Lord has created or with the way in which He moves with majesty and power.[23]

God the Father and His Son Jesus Christ are not students. They aren't making things up as they go. They are not conceiving new strategies because the adversary pulled a fast one on them.

God the Father and His Son Jesus Christ are not students. They aren't making things up as they go. They are not conceiving new strategies because the adversary pulled a fast one on them. We are not a test case, rats scurrying about in a great, cosmic lab. Referring to God, Elder Bruce R. McConkie said, "Why anyone should suppose that an infinite and eternal Being . . . who made the sidereal heavens, whose creations are more numerous than the particles of the earth, and who is aware of the fall of every sparrow—why anyone would suppose that such a Being has more to learn and new truths to discover in the laboratories of eternity is totally beyond my comprehension."[24]

Heavenly Father and the Savior are perfect. They know and understand *everything*, and they have all power. They are omnipotent, omniscient, and omnipresent. Further, the Atonement is not only infinite, it is perfect and perfectly personal. The Savior has already experienced all our griefs, sorrows, disappointments, and pains—completely and perfectly.

Our Father and His Son understand the adversary's tactics and motives perfectly, as well as the nature of the test we are all now taking. Therefore, They know what we need before we ask Them.[25] They know and see the end from the beginning.[26] Their motives, understanding, and love for us are perfect. They want us to become like They are—and every privilege and blessing They give us is designed to help us become the men and women we ultimately have the potential of becoming. In short, They want one thing: to see both Their sons and Their daughters progress to the point that we can live as They live and where They live.

Surely, then, They know how to structure our lives here, not to mention the Savior's Church, in a manner that will give all of us—men and women alike—the experiences, challenges, responsibilities, and opportunities best designed to qualify and prepare us for eternal life. The Prophet Joseph observed that "as God has designed our happiness—and the happiness of all His creatures, He never has—He never will institute an ordinance or give a commandment to His people that is not calculated in its nature to promote that happiness which He has designed, and which will not end in the greatest amount of good and glory to those who become the recipients of His law and ordinances."[27]

This point of view may seem unfathomable to some. But then, faith in God the Father and in His Son Jesus Christ will always seem crazy to the faithless.[28] Unbelievers never understand the beliefs of believers. They will always choose logic over faith. The problem with logic alone is that it confirms understanding and knowledge only to the limits of our feeble minds. One of Satan's great victories occurs when he manages to convince someone that his or her I.Q. is enough, that he or she has no need of help from God.

Those who don't believe in God or in His Son, or who don't believe that The Church of Jesus Christ of Latter-day Saints is in fact the Lord's Church, simply find it impossible to understand those who do.

But I believe. I *know* that the Lord's own Church, filled with His authority, power, and purpose, is on earth today, and that it *is* The Church of Jesus Christ of Latter-day Saints. Happily, this knowledge is available to every sincere, seeking man or woman.

The most fundamental belief of a member of The Church of Jesus Christ of Latter-day Saints is "that Jesus Christ is the Son of God, and that he was crucified for the sins of the world."[29] Building upon that knowledge is another fundamental belief—that The Church of Jesus Christ of Latter-day Saints *is* the Lord's Church, and that everything in it belongs to Him. That He presides. That the manner in which He authorizes the distribution of His authority and power throughout the earth is through priesthood keys. And that He selects who will have keys and then directs them to use those keys according to His will.[30]

Here is the beauty of these assertions: None of us has to take anyone else's word for them. Through personal revelation via the whisperings of the Spirit, we may *know for ourselves*[31] that God is our Father, that He is the author of the plan of salvation, and that He gave us His Only Begotten Son, Jesus Christ, so that each of us may have eternal life. We may *know for ourselves* that this is the Lord's Church. We may *know for ourselves* that there is a living prophet on earth today and that he holds and exercises all the keys of the Lord's priesthood. We may *know for ourselves* that Apostles of the Lord Jesus Christ, who also hold all priesthood keys, walk the earth today and minister to all who will listen. We may *experience for ourselves* the miracle of personal revelation and the peace and power of the house of the Lord. We may *know for ourselves* that the doctrine of the gospel, on any subject, is true and a reflection of the Lord's will. And we may *know for ourselves* that men and women are equal in the eyes of our Father and His Son, that our Father's daughters and sons have been given exactly what they need to propel them toward exaltation, and that anything other than that would be utterly inconsistent with who the Father and the Son are.

We may *know for ourselves* the truth of President Gordon B. Hinckley's declaration: "Do we as Latter-day Saints really understand and appreciate the strength of our position? Among the religions of the world, it is unique and wonderful. Is this Church an educational institution? Yes. We are constantly and endlessly teaching, teaching, teaching. . . . Is it a social organization? Indeed. It is a great family of friends who mingle together and enjoy one another. Is it a mutual aid society? Yes. It has a remarkable program for building self-reliance and granting aid to those in distress. It is all of these and more. But beyond these it is the Church and kingdom of God established and directed by our Eternal Father and His Beloved Son, the risen Lord Jesus Christ, to bless all who come within its fold."[32]

Surely in His infinite wisdom and perfect love, He has given His children—both men and women—the gifts, privileges, assignments, and challenges they need to learn to walk by faith and to eventually become exalted beings.

If the Lord's work and glory is to bring to pass the immortality and eternal life of man, *and it is*; if His entire purpose is to help us ultimately live where He lives and become as He is, *and it is*; then surely in His infinite wisdom and perfect love, He has given His children—both men and women—the gifts, privileges, assignments, and challenges they need to learn to walk by faith and to eventually become exalted beings.

President Henry B. Eyring said it this way: "This is the true Church of Jesus Christ. Only in the priesthood keys held by [the President of the Church] is the power for us to be sealed in families to live forever with our Heavenly Father and the Lord Jesus Christ. We will on the Day of Judgment stand before the Savior, face to face. It will be a time of joy for those who have drawn close to Him in His service in this life."[33]

God is perfect, and so is His plan for us. The Lord Jesus Christ is perfect, and He stands at the head of the Church. It is as President Harold B. Lee once told an audience of BYU students: "[The Savior] is closer to this church than you have any idea that he is."[34] The gospel of the Lord Jesus Christ, so central to our Father's plan, has been restored to the earth complete with all truth, all power, and all authority. That gospel is found in The Church of Jesus Christ of Latter-day Saints. Having a witness that this is true is foundational and fundamental to understanding how God sees and feels about His daughters and what their standing is in the kingdom of God.

Chapter 5

WOMEN ARE VITAL TO THE SUCCESS OF THE LORD'S CHURCH

Some time ago I was introduced to an accomplished woman of another faith—bright, articulate, generally well-informed about the issues of the day—whom I liked instantly. As we were getting acquainted, she said, "I have to tell you that I don't think much of your church."

"Really?" I responded. "Tell me why."

Her answer was straightforward: "Because women in your church aren't allowed to participate." I tried to keep a straight face but couldn't and started to laugh. She looked puzzled and asked what was so funny.

"If you told an audience of actively involved LDS women that you believed they didn't get to 'participate' in the Church, they would laugh right out loud and wonder how you had come up with that idea. Nothing could be further from the truth." Naturally, she wanted to know what women did in our Church, and that was all the encouragement I needed to give her a glimpse into life as an LDS woman.

I began by telling her about callings I'd had, beginning as an eighth grader when I was called to be the sacrament meeting pianist in our little Kansas branch, and then as a teenager when I served in the branch Primary presidency. I told her about serving as a ward Relief Society president at age twenty-four, then as a stake Relief Society president in a stake where almost every woman was married except for me, and then as a member of the Relief Society general board—and what those experiences had taught me about loving, teaching, and caring about women whose lives were different from mine. I told her about visiting teaching, serving in Young Women, teaching gospel doctrine and institute, and being a leader at girls camp and youth conference. And I briefly explained what my service in the Relief Society general presidency had entailed, including teaching and counseling with women around the world. "Does that sound to you as though I haven't been allowed to participate?" I asked, and then paused before adding: "The irony is that almost every opportunity I've ever had to learn and grow has come *because* of the Church, not in spite of it."[1] My new friend was surprised, and she admitted that though women were eligible for ordination in her church, there weren't nearly as many ways for women in general to contribute and participate.

> *Almost every opportunity I've ever had to learn and grow has come because of the Church, not in spite of it.*

WOMEN ARE INTEGRAL TO CHURCH LEADERSHIP

In The Church of Jesus Christ of Latter-day Saints, women are integral to Church leadership and governance. And because of the Church's lay leadership, actively participating members are all enrolled in what is essentially an ongoing leadership training program. A woman serving as a counselor in a stake Young Women presidency may next be called to teach Sunday School or Primary or to work in the library. One of the reasons Latter-day Saints can mobilize so quickly in times of disaster is that we learn to lead, and we also learn to follow. Over time, we learn how to do whatever the Lord needs us to do.

Latter-day Saint women have unusual influence and privileges in the Church, *many of which require ordination in other churches.* We pray, preach, and expound scriptures from the pulpit in sacrament meeting; lead, direct, and teach in organizations for all women, young women, and children in the Church; teach gospel doctrine in Sunday School to people of both genders and all ages; teach seminary and institute classes to teenagers and young adults of both genders; officiate in priesthood ordinances for women in the temple; participate with male leaders in significant Church councils on both the local and general levels; and at age nineteen are eligible to preach the gospel on proselyting missions throughout the world.

Latter-day Saint women have unusual influence and privileges in the Church, many of which require ordination in other churches.

Women hold all administrative and teaching offices in the Relief Society, which is now one of the oldest, largest, and most influential women's organizations in the world, numbering more than 6.5 million members in some 185 nations.[2] They also hold all administrative and teaching offices in the Young Women organization, which teaches and oversees all activities for teenage girls from ages twelve through seventeen. They preside over and fill most teaching assignments in the Primary, which provides Sunday instruction and other activities for children from ages three through eleven. And beyond these organizational roles, women are often at the center of gospel teaching, compassionate service, and humanitarian outreach.

In short, women hold about as many leadership positions in LDS congregations as men do. They deliver about as many sermons, hold roughly as many teaching positions (and perhaps more, considering the Primary organization, which is staffed largely by women), and oversee about as many service projects, activities, and programs as do men.

And all of this starts early. When three-year-olds enter Primary, they begin giving talks and offering prayers in meetings. Girls begin stepping into leadership positions at age twelve when they enter Young Women, and this continues for the rest of their lives. Teenage girls offer doctrinal messages in sacrament meeting and speak in other public settings, including testimony meeting, where they are free to express their convictions as they desire.

The remarkable training and experience Latter-day Saint women receive is just one of the reasons I have said before, and will say again, that you could take me to any country in the world where the Church is organized, give me a day, and I could find women who would hold their own with any group of women in the world. And that's a fact. Latter-day Saint women know how to organize, serve, inspire, and lead. They know how to "rise to the occasion," whatever the occasion may be.

Women are integral to building up the kingdom of God on earth. And they are also vital to its success.

THE FOUNDING OF THE RELIEF SOCIETY

Happily, none of these privileges are twenty-first-century conveniences, put in place for political expediency. The participation women enjoy in the Church today began in earnest in 1842, when Joseph Smith promised the women of the Church that he would organize them "after the pattern of the priesthood."[3] John Taylor, who attended the inaugural meeting of the Female Relief Society of Nauvoo on March 17, 1842, with Joseph, declared that the Prophet organized the women "according to the law of Heaven."[4]

Later that month, Joseph Smith visited Relief Society again, teaching the sisters that "the Society should move according to the ancient Priesthood" and explaining that the women of Relief Society must become a "select Society separate from all the evils of the world, choice, virtuous, and holy."[5]

The "ancient Priesthood" to which the Prophet referred is the higher or Melchizedek Priesthood, which provides all of us—men and women—with access to God's greatest blessings. These include the supernal privileges of having the "heavens opened unto [us]" and "receiving the mysteries of the kingdom of heaven," which the Lord defined as "the key of the knowledge of God."[6] So when Joseph Smith instructed the women to "move according to the ancient Priesthood," he was not only indicating the power under which the Relief Society would operate but inviting the sisters to prepare for sacred temple ordinances, which ordinances would bless them with an endowment of knowledge and power that would open the heavens to them. (This is discussed in greater depth in chapter 6.)

> *When Joseph Smith instructed the women to "move according to the ancient Priesthood," he was not only indicating the power under which the Relief Society would operate but inviting the sisters to prepare for sacred temple ordinances, which ordinances would bless them with an endowment of knowledge and power that would open the heavens to them.*

That Joseph managed to organize the Relief Society at all was remarkable. The year 1842 was not a tranquil time for him. He was contending with an endless parade of threats and accusations, ministering to a growing band of beleaguered Saints and immigrants, attempting to build a temple with meager resources, and leading a young Church through the intense, step-by-step, line-upon-line process of restoration.

Further, society at large was still highly patriarchal and, as such, strictly limiting of women's rights. Women couldn't vote, let alone hold office or even exert political influence. (The landmark Seneca Falls Convention, where the push for women's suffrage began in earnest, was still six years away.) Most women were denied higher education, and many weren't formally educated at all. Few had any way of earning money, and if a woman did earn a wage, it legally belonged to her husband. It was still unusual for women to own property. And some physical violence against women was not only tolerated socially but protected by law! The bottom line? In 1842, many still viewed women as being just a rung higher on the social ladder than prisoners.

Eliza R. Snow articulated the challenges women at large faced during that era: "The status of women," she wrote, "is one of the questions of the day. Socially and politically it forces itself upon the attention of the world. Some . . . refuse to concede that woman is entitled to the enjoyment of any rights other than those which the whims, fancies, or justice . . . of men may choose to grant her. The reasons (against treating women as equals) which (men) cannot meet with argument they decry and ridicule; an old refuge for those opposed to correct principles which they are unable to controvert."[7]

It was in stark contrast to the conventions of the day for the leader of an organization—*any* organization, not to mention the leader of a religion—to give women significant time and attention. If Joseph Smith had been taking his cues from his circumstances or the social or political climate, he likely would not have organized the women. But he was taking his direction from the Lord.

Not only did Joseph Smith organize the Relief Society, attend regularly, and repeatedly teach the women, he often took other Church leaders with him: Brigham Young, John Taylor, Heber C. Kimball, Willard Richards, and George A. Smith, to name a few. It is significant to note that in the first half of the nineteenth century, the Church's presiding leaders found women worth their time.

Simply put, the founding of the Relief Society is evidence of a people who believed in women and their influence and potential. It is the history of an organization destined to provide a framework for women to join together in influence—both in quiet, one-on-one ways and in contributions that affect communities, countries, and even continents for the better. It is the history of an organization destined to elevate women to their proper and appropriate standing. It is a history of vision.

The Relief Society champions womanhood and inspires its members to increase their personal righteousness and faith in God the Father and His Son Jesus Christ, to strengthen families and homes, and to seek out and help those in need through charitable outreach both at home and worldwide.

The founding of the Relief Society is evidence of a people who believed in women and their influence and potential. It is the history of an organization destined to elevate women to their proper and appropriate standing. It is a history of vision.

In 1945, then-Church President George Albert Smith put the organization of the Relief Society into perspective, telling LDS women, "You are . . . more blessed than any other women in all the world. You were the first women to have the franchise; the first women to have a voice in the work of a church. It was God that gave it to you and it came as a result of revelation to a Prophet of the Lord. Since that time, think what benefits the women of this world have enjoyed. Not only you belonging to the Church have enjoyed the blessing of equality, but when the Prophet Joseph Smith turned the key for the emancipation of womankind, it was turned for all the world, and from generation to generation the number of women who can enjoy the blessings of religious liberty and civil liberty has been increasing."[8]

Some skeptics have suggested that it took too long (twelve years from the organization of the Church in 1830) to organize the women in 1842. But that perspective is narrow at best. The "restoration of all things" relative to the Lord's Church was not simple, formulaic, neat and tidy, or quick.[9] Think of it—Joseph Smith was just fourteen when he had the First Vision and still a young adult (only twenty-four) when the Church was organized on April 6, 1830. He had never had nor been a bishop, never been a member of a priesthood quorum, never attended seminary or youth conference, never had a Church leader to nurture him along, never heard a prophet speak. He *was* the prophet. He had no precedent, no manuals, no handbook of instructions. He had to translate the Book of Mormon from an ancient record and then find a way to get it published. The revelations expounding doctrine that we turn to so readily in the Doctrine and Covenants had to be received one by one—by him. And everything he accomplished was against a backdrop of persistent persecution, opposition, apostasy of some he trusted most, and upheaval.

Counselors to Joseph Smith were not even called until 1832, the First Presidency was not organized until a year later, and the Quorum of the Twelve Apostles not until 1835. The first endowments were given in 1842, but vicarious endowments for the dead did not commence until January 1877 in the St. George Temple.[10] So despite the centrality to the plan of salvation of sealing generations to each other in the temple—which we understand so clearly now—it took nearly fifty years from the organization of the Church for all the ordinances necessary for eventual exaltation to be implemented. The burden of putting in place the myriad of privileges and blessings we enjoy today was borne by those who preceded us. We stand on the shoulders of men and women who had courageous hearts, indefatigable faith in Jesus Christ, and devotion to truth.

The Restoration took time, line upon line. It was, and is, ongoing. Women were not bystanders during the Restoration, and from the beginning they have not been bystanders in the Lord's kingdom.

A LEGACY OF SERVICE

Eve led the way when she took the step that freed men and women from eternal stagnation by making it possible for us to be born into mortality,[11] gain a body, and experience this period of probation. It is because of Eve's courageous act, and it is through her daughters, that every soul who receives a body is escorted through the veil that separates us here on earth from the premortal world. Even Jesus Christ, the Only Begotten of the Father, came to earth through the sacrifice of a woman.

Elder Dallin H. Oaks taught: "It was Eve who first transgressed the limits of Eden in order to initiate the conditions of mortality. Her act, whatever its nature, was formally a transgression but eternally a glorious necessity to open the doorway toward eternal life. Adam showed his wisdom by doing the same. And thus Eve and 'Adam fell that men might be' (2 Ne. 2:25). Some Christians condemn Eve for her act, concluding that she and her daughters are somehow flawed by it. Not the Latter-day Saints! Informed by revelation, we celebrate Eve's act and honor her wisdom and courage in the great episode called the Fall."[12]

> *Even Jesus Christ, the Only Begotten of the Father, came to earth through the sacrifice of a woman.*

It was Eve who uttered what is surely *the most* magnificent single-sentence sermon about our Father's plan for His children: "Were it not for our transgression we never should have had seed, and never should have known good and evil, and the joy of our redemption, and the eternal life which God giveth unto all the obedient."[13]

President James E. Faust declared that "we all owe a great debt of gratitude to Eve. . . . The choice [of Adam and Eve] was really between a continuation of their comfortable existence in Eden, where they would never have progress, or a momentous exit into mortality with its opposites; pain, trials, and physical death in contrast to joy, growth, and the potential for eternal life. . . . If it hadn't been for Eve, none of us would be here. . . . Mother Eve left a lasting legacy that comes down through the ages to bless the lives of all men and women."[14]

Surely "our glorious Mother Eve"[15] was one of the most revered of all our Father's spirit sons and daughters. Though Adam was ordained to the priesthood, he could not by himself fulfill the measure of his creation or further the purpose of the creation of the earth. Together Adam and Eve opened the way for us to continue to progress,[16] and in the process Eve established a righteous pattern for all women. She modeled what all faithful mothers do by facilitating the progression and growth of her children, which in her case includes all of us.

A host of magnificent women have followed in Eve's footsteps. Consider the following: Sarah had the faith to believe she could bear a child when she was past age, "because she judged him faithful who had promised."[17]

An inspired Egyptian woman responding to her maternal instincts retrieved the infant Moses from the bulrushes. In doing so, she spared the life of a future prophet and shaped all of history.

Deborah, regarded as a prophetess, judge, and mother in Israel (though there is no indication that she ever bore a child), was a catalyst who inspired an Israeli army to overcome Canaanite oppression.[18]

Esther summoned her faith, stood with courage, and saved a generation of her people.[19]

An impoverished widow whose son was starving taught us how to give and obey as she shared what she believed was her last meal and oil with Elijah.[20]

Though Adam was ordained to the priesthood, he could not by himself fulfill the measure of his creation or further the purpose of the creation of the earth. Together Adam and Eve opened the way for us to continue to progress, and in the process Eve established a righteous pattern for all women.

In order for the Savior to be born, there had to be a woman worthy of bearing Him. Ancient prophets foresaw the role of Mary, without whom the plan of salvation would have been thwarted, prophesying that the Savior would be born to a woman who was "a virgin, a precious and chosen vessel."[21] Gabriel appeared to her. Angelic choirs and voices attended the birth of her son, *the* Son of God.

A Samaritan woman drawing water at Jacob's Well was among the first in the New Testament record to hear the Savior declare who He was.[22] And it was not unusual for Him—though a departure from customs of the day—to teach women, as in the case of Mary and Martha.[23]

It was Martha to whom the Lord declared: "I am the resurrection, and the life. . . . And whosoever liveth and believeth in me shall never die. Believest thou this?" Martha responded with the kind of faith countless believing women have exemplified throughout the history of the world: "Yea, Lord: I believe that thou art the Christ, the Son of God."[24]

Matthew, Mark, Luke, and John each wrote about the women present during the final great episode of the Savior's mortal ministry—His Crucifixion and Resurrection. Women came from Galilee to Calvary and were "there beholding afar off, . . . ministering unto him,"[25] then followed His body to the sepulchre to witness "where he was laid."[26] Mary Magdalene, Joanna, Mary the mother of James, and other women returned to the tomb with spices and saw it empty.[27]

It was a woman who was the first mortal to see a resurrected Being—Mary of Magdala—and it was women whom the Lord instructed to carry the news of His Resurrection to His Apostles.[28] No wonder Elder James E. Talmage asserted that "the world's greatest champion of woman and womanhood is Jesus the Christ."[29]

THE LEGACY CONTINUES

Latter-day Saint women in this dispensation have proven their mettle just as did those in ancient times.

When Joseph Smith learned about everything the women were doing to help finish the interior of the Kirtland Temple, he told them, "The sisters are always first and foremost in all good works. Mary was first at the resurrection; and the sisters now are the first to work on the inside of the temple."[30]

Mary Ann Pratt is indicative of the strength and heroic faith LDS women have demonstrated from the early days of the Restoration. She married Elder Parley P. Pratt in 1837, moved to Missouri, and there suffered the persecutions that drove the Saints from county to county.

When her husband was later taken by a mob in Far West, Missouri, and imprisoned, Mary Ann was confined to bed with a raging fever—despite needing to care for an infant and a five-year-old. She pleaded with the Lord for help and eventually, miraculously, recovered.

Her health restored, Mary Ann visited her husband in jail, staying for a time with him there. She wrote: "I shared his dungeon, which was a damp, dark, filthy place, without ventilation, merely having a small grating on one side. In this we were obliged to sleep."

Eventually her husband was released, and she accompanied him on missions to New York and England. They were among those who made "the final weary gathering to Utah," as she described it. Elder Pratt ultimately died a martyr's death while serving yet another mission. Despite it all, Mary Ann maintained, "I was baptized into the Church of Jesus Christ of Latter-day Saints . . . being convinced of the truthfulness of its doctrines by the first sermon I heard; and I said in my heart, if there are only three who hold firm to the faith, I will be one of that number; and through all the persecution I have had to endure I have ever felt the same; my heart has never swerved from that resolve."[31]

> *"I said in my heart, if there are only three who hold firm to the faith, I will be one of that number; and through all the persecution I have had to endure I have ever felt the same; my heart has never swerved from that resolve."*
>
> —MARY ANN PRATT

More recently, Elder Quentin L. Cook related an experience he had at a stake conference in Tonga where the influence of women was powerfully evident. In that conference, the names of sixty-three prospective elders were sustained for ordination to the Melchizedek Priesthood. When Elder Cook asked how this many men had become ready and worthy for priesthood advancement at the same time, the stake president told him that in a particular stake council meeting where reactivation was being discussed, the stake Relief Society president, Sister Leinata Va'enuku, said there were many men in their late twenties and early thirties who had not served missions, who felt they had disappointed their priesthood leaders and families, and who felt like second-class citizens in the Church. She expressed love for these young men and suggested that the council focus on priesthood ordinations and temple ordinances for them. She noted that many of them had married wonderful women, though some of those women were less active or not members.

"As she spoke, the Spirit confirmed to the [stake] president that what she was suggesting was true," Elder Cook explained. "It was decided that the men of the priesthood and the women of the Relief Society would reach out to rescue these men and their wives. . . . During the next two years, almost all of the 63 men who had been sustained to the Melchizedek Priesthood at the stake conference I attended were endowed in the temple and had their spouses sealed to them. This account is but one example of how critical our sisters are in the work of salvation."[32]

Mary Ann Pratt, Leinata Va'enuku, and a host of other Latter-day Saint women have been living examples of President Heber J. Grant's statement that "without the wonderful work of . . . women, I realize that the Church would have been a failure."[33]

PERSONAL EXPERIENCE

I have experienced the joy of working hand in hand with priesthood and auxiliary leaders. I served as a young stake Relief Society president under the leadership of a stake president who extended a standing invitation for me to meet with him anytime I had a concern. One day I talked to him about an unproductive pattern I had observed in the working relationships between some bishops and their auxiliary presidents. He responded by inviting me to join him in addressing the subject at an upcoming bishops' training meeting. At the appointed hour, I arrived at the stake center and waited to be invited into the meeting.

When the door opened and I entered the high council room, the stake president quickly rose to his feet, and all the other men in the room followed suit. A wave of emotion rushed over me at this unexpected gesture of respect and inclusion. The stake president then motioned me toward the table where he and his counselors were sitting and said, "Sister Dew, please join us. We have a seat for you with us." He then said, "Brethren, I have invited Sister Dew to discuss a subject *we are both* concerned about. Please listen carefully to what she has to say." After I delivered the message, the stake president said in his remarks, "I endorse everything Sister Dew has taught and ask you to act on her suggestions. If you wish for her counsel in working with your sister leaders, please feel free to contact her." Many bishops followed through, and we counseled together on how to improve the working relationship between bishopric members and ward auxiliary leaders.

Imagine how I felt serving with a stake president who treated me as a trusted and valued member of his team. I would have walked barefoot on hot coals to help him accomplish the Lord's objectives for our stake!

That experience is literally one of hundreds that have demonstrated for me the power that results when priesthood leaders and auxiliary leaders unite in purpose and effort. Sister Julie B. Beck, former Relief Society general president, taught that "quorums and Relief Societies are an organized discipleship with the responsibility to assist in our Father's work to bring about eternal life for His children. We are not in the entertainment business; we are in the salvation business. . . . Where quorums and Relief Societies are unified in this work, they each essentially take an oar in the boat—each helping us move toward salvation."[34]

The experience of the stake in Tonga, mentioned earlier, exemplifies what happens when righteous men and women are unified in the work of salvation. The Relief Society president had the courage to speak clearly and candidly about a need she perceived. The stake president recognized the inspiration in her comments. Men holding the Melchizedek Priesthood and the women of Relief Society joined together in a united rescue effort, and the results were astonishing.

It is a wise priesthood leader who recognizes the value of sister leaders and expects and invites their full participation in a ward or stake council. And it is a wise auxiliary leader who learns how to speak up and be heard in a council without becoming domineering or inflexible and while always paying to those who hold priesthood keys the respect that those keys deserve.

A LEGACY OF DEVOTION

Women devoted to God and His Son, Jesus Christ, have from the beginning of time and throughout this dispensation demonstrated faith, devotion, and courage. They have participated in Church governance as well as in the grueling process of laying a foundation of faith that millions since have built upon. An episode in the life of Eliza R. Snow is representative of countless others.

It was December 1838 and one of the darkest times in the history of the Church, not to mention one of the coldest Decembers on record in Missouri. The Prophet Joseph Smith was imprisoned in Liberty Jail, and Governor Lilburn W. Boggs had issued an extermination order evicting all Latter-day Saints from the state, in the process unleashing the Missouri militia as well as freelance mobs upon Latter-day Saints living in particular in northern Missouri. Church members were fleeing the state, including Eliza and her father, mother, three brothers, sister, and two nieces.

It was bitter cold, the ground covered with snow. One evening the Snows stopped at a "halfway house," a log building twenty feet square where the fleeing homeless knew to look for a night's shelter. It was, however, a miserable situation. The chinkings between the logs were missing, most likely having been burned as firewood by earlier refugees, and the sharp north wind had free ingress through openings wide enough for cats to crawl through.

That particular night eighty people crowded into the log cabin. Most stood all night, though Eliza and her sister found a place for their mother to lie down along the wall. Eliza recorded that "the cold was so intense that, in spite of well packing, our food was frozen hard, bread and all, and although a blazing fire was burning on one side of the room, we could not get to it to thaw our suppers, and had to resort to the next expediency, which was this: The boys milked, and while one strained the milk, another held the pan . . . ; then, while one held a bowl of the warm milk, another would, as expeditiously as possible, thinly slice the frozen bread into it, and thus we managed for supper."

Meanwhile, the men built a roaring fire outside around which they stood and sang hymns all night while they parched corn and roasted frosted potatoes. Despite the conditions all around, Eliza's description of the evening was cheery: "Not a complaint was heard—all were cheerful, and judging from appearance, strangers would have taken us to be pleasure excursionists rather than a band of gubernatorial exiles." A postscript was likewise enlightening: "But, withal, that was a very merry night. None but saints can be happy under every circumstance."

She identified the source of their optimism: "It is true our hardships and privations were sufficient to have disheartened any but the saints of the living God—those who were prompted by higher than earthly motives, and trusting in the arm of Jehovah."[35]

From Eve to Mary Ann Pratt, from Eliza to Leinata Va'enuku, women of God have faced hardships they couldn't possibly have imagined and in the process bequeathed a spiritual heritage to those who followed them. President Joseph F. Smith described this heritage when he said to the women of the Relief Society in 1914: "It is not for you to be led by the women of the world; it is for you to . . . lead the women of the world in everything that is praiseworthy, everything that is God-like, everything that is uplifting and . . . purifying to the children of men."[36]

Elder John A. Widtsoe taught that women bear "joint responsibility with [men] in establishing the Kingdom of God." He added that "the work will fail unless both do their duty."[37]

Not only do Latter-day Saint women participate in the Church, they are integral to its vitality and governance.

Chapter 6

BOTH WOMEN AND MEN HAVE ACCESS TO GOD'S HIGHEST SPIRITUAL BLESSINGS

President David O. McKay once posed the question to the members of the Church, "If at this moment each one of you were asked to state in one sentence or phrase the most distinguishing feature of The Church of Jesus Christ of Latter-day Saints, what would be your answer?" He then answered his own question, stating simply, the "divine authority of the priesthood."[1]

In the hierarchy of what is important in the Church, the priesthood—including priesthood keys, priesthood authority, and priesthood power—is at the top. "Not only is the priesthood the power by which the heavens and earth were created," said Elder M. Russell Ballard, "but it is also the power the Savior used in His mortal ministry to perform miracles, to bless and heal the sick, to bring the dead to life, and, as our Father's Only Begotten Son, to endure the unbearable pain of Gethsemane and Calvary. . . . During the glorious days of the Restoration and the reestablishment of the Church of Jesus Christ in the world today, John the Baptist; Peter, James, and John; Moses; Elias; and Elijah came to the earth and restored through the Prophet Joseph Smith all of the keys and authority of the priesthood for the work of God in these latter days."[2]

Nephi saw in vision how crucial God's power would be fo us living now, in the latter days: "I, Nephi, beheld the power of the Lamb of God, that it descended upon the saints of the church of the Lamb, and upon the covenant people of the Lord, who were scattered upon all the face of the earth; and they were armed with righteousness and with the *power of God in great glory*."[3]

In the world's vernacular and frame of reference, the word *power* typically evokes—or at least results in—domination and control, both of which are often used and abused for personal gain. And the thirst for power rarely has a righteous end. "Some sincerely wish for more power to do good," said Elder Neal A. Maxwell, "but only a few individuals are good enough to be powerful. But craving power and the spotlight sucks out the spiritual oxygen, leaving some 'past feeling.' . . . Those who bestow the transitory things of the world are, themselves, transients. They cannot confer that which is lasting because they do not possess it."[4]

In illuminating contrast, God's power is about unity rather than control and domination. God makes His power available to His covenant-making children so that they can become one with Him and one with each other. When we enter the waters of baptism, we not only covenant to serve God and keep His commandments, we promise to bear one another's burdens, to mourn with those who mourn, and to comfort those who need comfort. When we receive the Holy Ghost, we have the capacity to know all things the Lord would have us do and to gradually, increasingly become one with Him. When we are endowed, we bind ourselves more fully to the Lord, and He binds Himself to us. When we enter the new and everlasting covenant of marriage, we take an essential step to ultimately becoming like our Father and His Son—to having no end, living from everlasting to everlasting, and having all power.[5]

There are countless evidences that God actually wants a powerful people. An eight-year-old may receive the gift and power of the Holy

Ghost[6] and thus the privilege of constant access to the third member of the Godhood. A twelve-year-old boy may be ordained to the Aaronic Priesthood, which holds the "key of the ministering of angels and the preparatory gospel."[7] Every adult who qualifies may enter the house of the Lord, where he or she has the opportunity to "grow up" in the Lord, "receive a fulness of the Holy Ghost," and emerge armed with power and knowledge.[8] In a multitude of ways, the Lord has made it clear that He desires to have a righteous, pure people who both qualify for and seek to have access to His power, which by definition is priesthood power.

> *In a multitude of ways, the Lord has made it clear that He desires to have a righteous, pure people who both qualify for and seek to have access to His power, which by definition is priesthood power.*

With the indisputable significance of priesthood established, the statement that LDS women are eligible for the Lord's highest spiritual blessings, and yet ineligible for priesthood ordination, may strike some as confusing if not misleading. Some who feel concern over what they see as a blatant inequity have asked the question, "If Mormon men are the only ones eligible for the high privilege of priesthood ordination, what *do* Mormon women get?"

That is a fair question.

Elder Bruce R. McConkie taught that "where spiritual things are concerned, as pertaining to all of the gifts of the Spirit, with reference to the receipt of revelation, the gaining of testimonies, and the seeing of visions, in all matters that pertain to godliness and holiness and which are brought to pass as a result of personal righteousness—in all these things men and women stand in a position of absolute equality before the Lord."[9] This is reassuring doctrine, but what does it actually mean for LDS women?

THE CHALLENGE OF UNDERSTANDING AND DISCUSSING PRIESTHOOD

Understanding priesthood is not a simple matter for anyone, for several reasons. First, we tend to use the word *priesthood* in a variety of ways. Often it is used to refer to men, meaning to those who are ordained to the priesthood. How many times have you heard a conducting officer in sacrament meeting say, "We thank the Aaronic Priesthood for administering the sacrament"? It would be more fitting to say, "We thank those who hold the Aaronic Priesthood for administering the sacrament." The "Aaronic Priesthood" is not ordained teenage boys. It is the power and authority of the "lesser" priesthood.[10] Likewise, the Melchizedek Priesthood is not ordained men and is not synonymous with men or male administration. It is the power and authority of the "higher" priesthood.[11]

We actually diminish priesthood power when we equate it with *holders of the priesthood*. Elder Dallin H. Oaks explained that "some of our abbreviated expressions, like 'the women and the priesthood,' convey an erroneous idea. Men are not 'the priesthood.'"[12] Elder M. Russell Ballard spoke similarly: "In our Heavenly Father's great priesthood-endowed plan, men have the unique responsibility to administer the priesthood, but they are not the priesthood."[13]

Statements such as, "We would like to thank the priesthood for setting up chairs," or "I'm so grateful to have the priesthood in my home," are actually misleading and to some degree undermining of God's power. Priesthood *holders* are men. "The priesthood" refers to keys, authority, and power—God's power.

> *We actually diminish priesthood power when we equate it with* holders of the priesthood.

Second, we use the word *priesthood* interchangeably and often without clarification—meaning we use it to mean different things in different applications. Even prophets, seers, and revelators have used the word *priesthood* to mean different things at different times. Sometimes the word refers to keys without explicitly saying so; sometimes to authority; sometimes to power; sometimes to blessings; and sometimes to priesthood holders or leaders. In fact, different important statements from Church leaders cited in this very chapter use the term *priesthood* in varying applications.

Simply stated, priesthood is the power of God. It is the all-encompassing power by which He works. It is the power by which He creates, changes, and ultimately redeems us. It is beyond the beginning of days or end of years. It is the "power, by faith, to break mountains, to divide the seas, to dry up waters, to turn them out of their course; to put at defiance the armies of nations, to divide the earth, . . . to stand in the presence of God; to do all things according to his will."[14] In many respects, priesthood is beyond our comprehension, which leads to the next point of potential confusion.

Third, understanding the doctrine of the priesthood is not a simple matter for anyone, as Elder Bruce R. McConkie explained: "This doctrine of the priesthood—*unknown in the world* and but *little known even in the Church*—cannot be learned out of the scriptures alone. It is not set forth in the sermons and teachings of the prophets and Apostles, except in small measure. *The doctrine of the priesthood is known only by personal revelation.* It comes, line upon line and precept upon precept, by the power of the Holy Ghost to those who love and serve God with all their heart, might, mind, and strength. . . . Priesthood is power like none other on earth or in heaven."[15]

When we speak of the holy Melchizedek Priesthood, we are referring to the greatest power in heaven or on earth. Just as the doctrine of this priesthood can only be fully understood through revelation, understanding the relationship of women and priesthood requires the same.

There are four key truths related to women and priesthood that are crucial for both men and women to understand.

1. The Father's plan and the Savior's Church are designed to qualify all of us—both men and women—for exaltation.

---

2. Priesthood keys are the manner through which the Lord authorizes and disperses His power and authority throughout the Church for both men and women.

---

3. In the temple, both men and women are "endowed with the same power, which by definition is priesthood power."[16]

---

4. Neither a man nor a woman may receive the highest ordinances of the priesthood or be exalted alone.

1. The Father's Plan and the Savior's Church Are Designed to Qualify All of Us for Exaltation

It bears repeating from chapter 4 that the work and glory of the Father and the Son—and Their *sole* motivation—is to help us grow and progress so that we ultimately live *where* They live, *as* They live, and become *as* They are.

Our Father and His Son are not experimenting with us, hoping against hope that somehow things work out well for the human family. Their understanding and motives are perfect. Their understanding of each of us individually and of everything we will encounter in mortality is perfect. As Elder Tad R. Callister asked, "Could you ever imagine the Lord having a problem He could not solve?"[17]

Surely, then, our omniscient Father gave both His sons and His daughters the exact gifts, talents, privileges, responsibilities, opportunities, challenges, and divine errands we would need to help us stretch, struggle, serve, and eventually qualify for the gift of exaltation. To presume that we know better than our Father how to best prepare the human family for exaltation is absurd.

Every man and every woman who is serious about sanctification and who desires exaltation needs to come to understand and respect priesthood keys, authority, and power.

President Boyd K. Packer taught that "a man who holds the priesthood does not have an advantage over a woman in qualifying for exaltation. The woman, by her very nature, is also co-creator with God. . . . Virtues and attributes upon which perfection and exaltation depend come naturally to a woman."[18]

> *Every man and every woman who is serious about sanctification and who desires exaltation needs to come to understand and respect priesthood keys, authority, and power.*

This is all fine and good, say some who are concerned about what they perceive as second-class status for women in the Church. But does ordination for males, and lack of ordination for females, create a fundamentally unequal relationship between men and women? Does this place women at the ultimate mercy of men? Does it say something about how God sees His children? And why aren't women eligible for priesthood ordination anyway?

From my point of view, the answers to these questions are: No. No. No. And we don't know. Elder M. Russell Ballard said it well when he declared, "Does the Lord respect women? Do women matter to the Lord? The answer is yes—a resounding yes! . . . There are those who suggest that males are favored of the Lord because they are ordained to hold the priesthood. Anyone who believes this does not understand the great plan of happiness. The premortal and mortal natures of men and women were specified by the Lord Jehovah Himself, and it is simply not within His character to diminish the roles and responsibilities of any of [Heavenly Father's] children."[19]

On another occasion, Elder Ballard added: "Men and women have different but equally valued roles. Just as a woman cannot conceive a child without a man, so a man cannot fully exercise the power of the priesthood to establish an eternal family without a woman. . . . In the eternal perspective, both the procreative power and the priesthood power are shared by a husband and wife."[20]

President Gordon B. Hinckley explained that it was the Lord, not man, "who designated that men in His Church should hold the priesthood," and that it was also the Lord who endowed women with "capabilities to round out this great and marvelous organization, which is the Church and kingdom of God."[21]

Elder Neal A. Maxwell admitted that "we know so little . . . about the reasons for the division of duties between womanhood and manhood as well as between motherhood and priesthood. These were divinely determined in another time and another place. We are accustomed to focusing on the men of God because theirs is the priesthood and leadership line. But paralleling that authority line is a stream of righteous influence reflecting the remarkable women of God who have existed in all ages and dispensations, including our own. . . . Just as certain men were foreordained from before the foundations of the world, so were certain women appointed to certain tasks. Divine design—not chance—brought Mary forward to be the mother of Jesus. The boy prophet, Joseph Smith, was blessed . . . with a superb mother, Lucy Mack, who influenced a whole dispensation. . . . When the real history of mankind is fully disclosed, will . . . what happened in cradles and kitchens prove to be more controlling than what happened in congresses?"[22]

There are two reasons I am not troubled about the fact that we don't have clear answers for some issues involving women. First, because God is perfect, and His love for us is perfect, I have faith that His distribution of divine errands is perfectly constructed for the benefit of both His daughters and His sons as well as for the benefit and well-being of the Church.

Second, as Elder Jeffrey R. Holland declared, *"In this Church, what we know will always trump what we do not know. And remember, in this world, everyone is to walk by faith."*[23]

When all is said and done, we don't know the definitive reason the Lord divided assignments, divine gifts, privileges, and responsibilities between men and women the way He did. He has not seen fit to reveal or explain everything to us. But men and women of faith are required to *have* faith.

With the witness of the Spirit that God is our Father, that Jesus is the Christ, and that The Church of Jesus Christ of Latter-day Saints is truly the Lord's Church comes a confidence and sense of peace about the manner in which the Lord has organized His Church and the plan our Father has for us.

> *Because God is perfect, and His love for us is perfect, I have faith that His distribution of divine errands is perfectly constructed for the benefit of both His daughters and His sons as well as for the benefit and well-being of the Church.*

"The Family: A Proclamation to the World" clarifies vital truths about the fundamental division of roles between men and women: "By divine design, fathers are to preside over their families in love and righteousness and are responsible to provide the necessities of life and protection for their families. Mothers are primarily responsible for the nurture of their children. In these sacred responsibilities, fathers and mothers are obligated to help one another as equal partners."

Following this basic pattern in the primary responsibilities of men and women, the Lord has declared His will regarding the assignments men and women assume in Church governance. While women direct the affairs of the Primary, Young Women, and Relief Society, they are not assigned to assume ultimate direction of the ecclesiastical affairs of the Church, whereas men are. And as previously stated, although women are not ordained to the priesthood, they do have authority to officiate in priesthood ordinances in the temple.

On the other hand, women, unlike men, are not required to be ordained to the Melchizedek Priesthood in order to enter the house of the Lord, though the ordinances performed there are *all* priesthood ordinances. Neither are women required to be ordained to the priesthood to serve as leaders in the Lord's Church. Why is this the case? We don't know the answer to these questions, either. These are questions that at present may be answered only through personal revelation.

Some who believe women should be ordained to the priesthood point to statements by the Prophet Joseph Smith in which he implied that women could participate in priesthood blessings. As just one example, he stated in a sermon to Relief Society sisters in Nauvoo that there was no more sin in a "female laying hands on the sick than in wetting the face with water—that it is no sin for anybody to do it that has faith." He also "offered instruction respecting the propriety of females administering to the sick by the laying on of hands—said it was according to revelation."[24]

What are we to make of the fact that these statements don't square with Church doctrine and practice today? I don't know why the Prophet Joseph appears to have sanctioned females blessing the sick, though I've pondered different possibilities: Were these statements recorded accurately? Was the Prophet's reference to "administering to the sick" referring to prayers of faith and comfort rather than a priesthood ordinance? Had issues regarding women and priesthood not yet

Women, unlike men, are not required to be ordained to the Melchizedek Priesthood in order to enter the house of the Lord, though the ordinances performed there are all *priesthood ordinances. Neither are women required to be ordained to the priesthood to serve as leaders in the Lord's Church.*

been fully revealed? Was he anticipating women officiating in priesthood ordinances in the temple? Were there reasons the Lord allowed women to give blessings of healing—as distinct from performing actual ordinances—during those turbulent days in Nauvoo when illness threatened the Saints constantly, priesthood bearers were frequently away from home, and women often found themselves caring for their families alone? I don't know if any of these explanations are correct, though all would seem to be possibilities.

Elder Dallin H. Oaks has cautioned us to "remember that in those earliest days in Church history more revelation was to come. Thus, when he spoke to the sisters about the appropriateness of their laying on hands to bless one another, the Prophet cautioned, 'that the time had not been before that these things could be in their proper order—that the Church is not now organized in its proper order, and cannot be until the Temple is completed.' (*Minutes*, 28 Apr. 1842, p. 36.) During the century that followed, as temples became accessible to most members, 'proper order' required that these and other sacred practices be confined within those temples."[25]

LDS WOMEN LEAD, TEACH, TESTIFY, PRAY, AND EXPOUND DOCTRINE

As mentioned earlier, Latter-day Saint women participate in the Church in ways that require ordination in most other churches, and they do so from the most visible pulpits in the Church—including general conference.

This sweeping truth notwithstanding, there are those who feel that the participation and visibility of women need to increase. Others have had unfortunate experiences with priesthood leaders or priesthood bearers. Still others are troubled because within the Church's hierarchical structure, men ultimately control everything. "Men make the rules and they enforce the rules," is how some express it.[26]

It is true that examples of sexism can be found in the Church. As of this writing there are nearly fifteen million Church members who represent most of the world's cultures. Among that group, unfortunately, are some men who abuse power and therefore some women who have been oppressed.

But is sexism—or, heaven forbid, abuse of women—condoned by or inherent within the Church? Absolutely not. Does The Church of Jesus Christ of Latter-day Saints undermine or restrict the progression of women? The answer is a resounding "No!" In fact, Church doctrine declares exactly the opposite.

President Spencer W. Kimball admonished priesthood leaders that "our sisters do not wish to be indulged or to be treated condescendingly; they desire to be respected and revered as our sisters and our equals. I mention [this], my brethren, not because the doctrines or the teachings of the Church regarding women are in any doubt, but because in some situations our behavior is of doubtful quality."[27]

On a personal note, I have had splendid experiences with priesthood bearers and priesthood leaders—far too many to count. I have also occasionally had bewildering experiences with priesthood leaders. But does a difficult experience with a priesthood leader mean that priesthood authority isn't real or that there is something inherently wrong with the way the Lord has organized His Church? Of course not! (It is important to note that I have also had unpleasant experiences with female auxiliary leaders, and I shudder to think about those who have had difficult moments with me.) We

Does a difficult experience with a priesthood leader mean that priesthood authority isn't real or that there is something inherently wrong with the way the Lord has organized His Church? Of course not! We are mortals serving in a lay Church, and even the finest leaders have days when they don't handle authority particularly well. Human weakness is a reality in a lay ministry.

are mortals serving in a lay Church, and even the finest leaders have days when they don't handle authority particularly well. Human weakness is a reality in a lay ministry.

Elder Jeffrey R. Holland put it this way: "Be kind regarding human frailty—your own as well as those who serve with you in a Church led by volunteer, mortal men and women. Except in the case of His only perfect Begotten Son, imperfect people are all God has ever had to work with. That must be terribly frustrating to Him, but He deals with it. So should we. And when you see imperfection, remember that the limitation is *not* in the divinity of the work."[28] Or as Moroni said when finishing his father Mormon's work, "If there be faults they be the faults of a man."[29]

Years ago, Elder Marvin J. Ashton of the Quorum of the Twelve said to me in a moment of private mentoring, "Sheri, don't ever allow yourself to be offended by someone who is learning his job." It took a while for me to realize how comprehensive his counsel was, because as lay servant-leaders whose jobs rotate regularly, most of us are often in the process of "learning our jobs." Elder Ashton's wisdom has helped me look past difficult episodes and learn from rather than agonize over them.

When all is said and done, it is the Lord—not man—who ultimately controls everything. We are all dependent—women and men alike—upon priesthood leaders who hold priesthood keys exercising those keys and their authority righteously and as the Lord dictates.

Within this pattern of governance, LDS women have extraordinary opportunities for influence as leaders in the Church and teachers of the gospel. We truly do expound the gospel and exhort the Saints from pulpits across the Church.

A DEFINING TEST

Despite the fact that we do not yet know all things, we *do* know that our Father is the author of His plan for us and that His plan is perfect. We know that the Savior's Church, filled with His power and authority, has been restored to the earth to help us grow and progress. And we know that the overarching aim of our Father's plan and the Savior's Church is to help us understand who we are, why we are here, and who we may ultimately become.

It may well be that some of the *most* defining tests of mortality involve issues that swirl around gender, including how men feel about and treat women; how women feel about and treat men; how men feel about manhood and women about womanhood; and how all regard and honor priesthood keys, priesthood authority and priesthood power. Having a witness that Heavenly Father's plan and the Lord's Church are perfectly constructed to give us the maximum potential for achieving our eternal destiny is foundational to passing these tests.

2. Priesthood Keys Are the Manner through which the Lord Authorizes and Disperses His Power and Authority throughout the Church for Both Men and Women

It is crucial for men and women alike to understand the distinctions between priesthood keys, priesthood authority, and priesthood power. To set the stage, let's look at how keys, authority, and power work together to bless and change lives.

First example: In order for a worthy, Melchizedek Priesthood-bearing father to baptize and confirm his daughter, he must receive authorization to do so from his bishop, who holds the keys for his ward. The father, who by virtue of his ordination to the priesthood has the authority to perform ordinances when authorized by one who has keys, may then baptize his daughter, confirm her a member of the Church, and bestow upon her the gift of the Holy Ghost. Once the girl has been baptized, confirmed, and has received the Holy Ghost, she has direct access to the third member of the Godhead and may learn to receive

> *It is crucial for men and women alike to understand the distinctions between priesthood keys, priesthood authority, and priesthood power.*

personal revelation—which means she may benefit directly and individually from the blessings of priesthood power.

Second example: A worthy, Melchizedek Priesthood-bearing father cannot confer the Melchizedek Priesthood upon his son and ordain him an elder until a bishop, who has keys, and a stake president, who has keys, proclaim the son worthy to receive the Melchizedek Priesthood and until the stake president authorizes the father to perform the ordination. When that authorization occurs, the father, who has the authority to perform ordinances by virtue of his ordination to the Melchizedek Priesthood, may ordain his son. At that point, the son, now having received the priesthood, has authority to officiate in the ordinances of the Melchizedek Priesthood when authorized to do so by one who has keys. He also has direct access to the privileges and blessings and power of the priesthood.

Third example: In order for a woman to go to the temple, she must be authorized to do so by her bishop and stake president, both of whom have keys. Once they authorize her to enter the temple, she receives priesthood ordinances from those who have the authority to administer them—which in the temple includes both men and women. Having received those ordinances, she then has the privilege of having direct access to priesthood power for her own life and responsibilities. The challenge for her at that point is to learn how to access that power. (More will be said about this later in the chapter.)

To summarize the above three examples:

Worthy priesthood bearers are not able to perform saving ordinances without the authorization of those who hold priesthood keys.

Priesthood keys authorize saving ordinances.

Priesthood authority is required to perform those ordinances.

Priesthood power is available to all who receive those ordinances.

PRIESTHOOD KEYS

Priesthood keys are the "right of presidency,"[30] the right to "preside over and direct the work."[31] They are "the authority God has given to priesthood leaders to direct, control, and govern the use of His priesthood on earth. The exercise of priesthood authority is governed by those who hold its keys (see D&C 65:2; 81:2; 124:123). Those who hold priesthood keys have the right to preside over and direct the Church within a jurisdiction."[32]

By definition, keys open things. "All priesthood authority *in the Church* functions under the direction of the one who holds the appropriate priesthood keys,"[33] explained Elder Dallin H. Oaks.

Just because a man has been ordained to the priesthood does not mean he holds priesthood keys. In fact, most priesthood bearers do *not* have priesthood keys. At any given time, a relative few hold keys. The First Presidency and Quorum of the Twelve Apostles hold all keys of the Melchizedek Priesthood. *Handbook 2:*

Priesthood keys authorize saving ordinances.

Priesthood authority is required to perform those ordinances.

Priesthood power is available to all who receive those ordinances.

Administering the Church explains others who receive keys: "Seventies act by assignment and by the delegation of authority from the First Presidency and Quorum of the Twelve Apostles. Area Presidents are assigned to administer areas under the authorization of the First Presidency and the Twelve. The Presidency of the Seventy are set apart and are given the keys to preside over the Quorums of Seventy.

"The President of the Church delegates priesthood keys to other priesthood leaders so they can preside in their areas of responsibility. Priesthood keys are bestowed on presidents of temples, missions, stakes, and districts; bishops; branch presidents; and quorum presidents. This presiding authority is valid only for the designated responsibilities and within the geographic jurisdiction of each leader's calling."[34]

Though women do not hold priesthood keys, they do have opportunities to preside, as Elder Dallin H. Oaks clarified: "Under the priesthood authority of the bishop, the president of a ward Relief Society presides over and directs the activities of the Relief Society in the ward. A stake Relief Society president presides and exercises authority over the function to which she has been called. The same is true for the other auxiliaries. Similarly, women called as missionaries are set apart to go forth with authority to teach the everlasting gospel, and women called to work in a temple are given authority for the sacred functions to which they have been called. All function under the direction of the priesthood leader who has been given the priesthood keys to direct those who labor in his area of responsibility."[35]

Men and women alike receive authority to serve under the direction of a priesthood leader who holds keys. Those who hold priesthood keys authorize and open the flow of priesthood power in behalf of all who serve under their direction.

Men and women alike receive authority to serve under the direction of a priesthood leader who holds keys. Those who hold priesthood keys authorize and open the flow of priesthood power in behalf of *all* who serve under their direction.

In an epistle to the Church that is now canonized, the Prophet Joseph Smith taught how all-encompassing priesthood keys are: "It may seem to some to be a very bold doctrine that we talk of—a power which records or binds on earth and binds in heaven. Nevertheless, in all ages of the world, whenever the Lord has given a dispensation of the priesthood to any man by actual revelation, or any set of men, this power has always been given. . . . And again, for the precedent, Matthew 16:18, 19: *And I say also unto thee, that thou art Peter, and upon this rock I will build my church; and the gates of hell shall not prevail against it. And I will give unto thee the keys of the kingdom of heaven: and whatsoever thou shalt bind on earth shall be bound in heaven; and whatsoever thou shalt loose on earth shall be loosed in heaven.* Now the great and grand secret of the whole matter, and the *summum bonum* of the whole subject that is lying before us, consists in obtaining the powers of the Holy Priesthood. For him to whom these keys are given there is no difficulty in obtaining a knowledge of facts in relation to the salvation of the children of men."[36]

PRIESTHOOD AUTHORITY

Priesthood authority is conferred through ordination by the laying on of hands and is required to perform all sacred and saving ordinances.[37] "Through the authority of the Melchizedek Priesthood," states *Handbook 2: Administering the Church,* "Church leaders guide the Church, direct the preaching of the gospel throughout the world, and administer all the spiritual work of the Church."[38]

Elder Bruce R. McConkie explained the distinction between priesthood keys and priesthood authority. "Every elder . . . has the power to baptize, but no elder can use this power unless he is authorized to do so by someone holding the keys."[39]

Men and women alike receive and are blessed by the ordinances of salvation. President Boyd K. Packer taught that "the mariner gets his bearing from light coming from celestial bodies—the sun by day, the stars by night. . . . The spiritual sextant, which each of us has, also functions on the principle of light from celestial sources. Set that sextant in your mind to the word *covenant* or the word *ordinance*. The light will come through. Then you can fix your position and set a true course in life. No matter what citizenship or race, whether male or female, no matter what occupation, no matter your education, regardless of the generation in which one lives, life is a homeward journey for all of us, back to the presence of God in His celestial kingdom. Ordinances and covenants become our credentials for admission into His presence. To worthily receive them is the quest of a lifetime; to keep them thereafter is the challenge of mortality."[40]

Ordinances provide all who partake worthily with access to the power of God. With the exception of women who serve as ordinance workers in the temple, however, only men have the authority to officiate in the ordinances of the priesthood.

Though women do not hold priesthood keys and are not ordained with priesthood authority, this is not to say that they don't have opportunities to exercise authority, because they do.

President Joseph Fielding Smith taught that when Joseph Smith "turn[ed] the key" in behalf of women, he opened to them the privilege of exercising "some measure of divine authority, particularly in the direction of government and instruction in behalf of the women of the Church."[41] On another occasion, President Smith added, "While the sisters have not been given the Priesthood, . . . that does not mean that the Lord has not given unto them authority. Authority and Priesthood are two different things. A person may have authority given to him, or a sister to her, to do certain things in the Church that are binding and absolutely necessary for our salvation, such as the work that our sisters do in the House of the Lord."[42]

It is worth repeating that priesthood authority is required to perform all sacred and saving ordinances.

PRIESTHOOD POWER

Priesthood power is the power of God that emanates from the priesthood. Priesthood power and blessings are as available to worthy women (particularly endowed women) as to men. (More will be said under point 3 in this chapter about the ways in which women have direct access to priesthood power.)

As early as 1842, the Prophet Joseph Smith sought to teach women about the priesthood, and particularly about the priesthood power that would be available to them in the temple. In a Relief Society meeting held on April 28, 1842, he explained that the purpose of "his being present . . . was, to make observations respecting the Priesthood."[43] He then delivered a message that has at times been misinterpreted or misunderstood because he used the word *keys* in *two ways:* first, by referring to priesthood keys, which he exercised in behalf of the sisters; and second, by referring to the keys of knowledge and power that provide those who are endowed in the temple with direct access to God.

When Joseph organized the Relief Society and declared, "I now turn the key to you in the name of God and this Society shall rejoice and knowledge and intelligence shall flow down from this time,"[44] he was exercising priesthood keys in behalf of women and formally opening for them the privilege of serving, leading, and teaching in the Church.[45]

Elder Dallin H. Oaks taught that "when he 'turn[ed] the key,' the Prophet Joseph Smith made the Relief Society an official part of the Church and kingdom of God. This opened to women new opportunities for receiving knowledge and intelligence from on high, such as through the temple ordinances that were soon to be instituted. . . . No priesthood keys were delivered to the Relief Society. Keys are conferred on individuals, not organizations."[46]

It is important to note, however, that because Relief Society leaders serve under the direction of those who hold priesthood keys, they have the authority to preside over an organization that has the power to bless and strengthen lives that no other organization for women can claim.

The second way in which the Prophet used the word *keys* in his April 28 sermon to the Relief Society referred to keys of knowledge and power obtained by those endowed in the temple.[47] In this usage, the Prophet was not referring to priesthood keys held by priesthood leaders, and he was not suggesting that Relief Society leaders would receive priesthood keys. He was indicating that the "keys" that enable us to "detect everything false"—that is, the keys of knowledge and power given to the endowed—would be given to women as well as men. These keys provide access to heaven—to godly power, to personal revelation, and to heavenly help.

Sarah Rich, who labored with her husband in the Nauvoo Temple from seven a.m. until midnight each day for many weeks prior to their journey across the plains, recorded: "Many were the blessings we had received in the house of the Lord which has caused us joy and comfort in the midst of all our sorrows and enabled us to have faith in God, knowing he would guide us and sustain us in the unknown journey that lay before us. For if it had not been for the faith and knowledge that was bestowed upon us in that temple by the influence and help of the Spirit of the Lord, our journey would have been like one taking a leap in the dark."[48]

The Prophet Joseph taught the women the doctrine of the priesthood, organized them after the pattern of the priesthood, and taught them that this pattern would soon be evident in the highest priesthood ordinances conferred in the temple. In other words, he organized women in a manner that would allow them to work officially and cooperatively with priesthood leaders in helping administer the Church and build up the kingdom of God, a pattern mirroring the divine pattern of the celestial union of man and woman required for exaltation.

UNDERSTANDING PRIESTHOOD AND WOMEN

For as long as I can remember, the exercise of the priesthood has moved me. Even as a girl, I knew that priesthood power was real—that it really was the power and authority of God, and that it really would bless, heal, protect, and strengthen me.

Perhaps for that reason, I've never been troubled about women not being ordained. But along the way, I have found myself serving women who *were* troubled and burdened with the misconception that a lack of ordination for women is proof positive that women are not as valued as men by the Lord or at least by His Church. Because of this, there came a time when I realized that a testimony of the divinity of priesthood was not enough. I needed to understand the doctrine of the priesthood so that I could better understand the connection between priesthood and women.

Women need to understand priesthood power just as much as men do.

The desire to understand more about the priesthood sent me to the scriptures. I studied passages on priesthood over and over again. Sections 20, 76, 84, 107, 121, and 124 of the Doctrine and Covenants; JST, Genesis 14:25–40; JST, Hebrews 7; and Alma 13 became dog-eared in my scriptures. I wanted to understand what priesthood keys are, and what the distinction is between priesthood keys, priesthood authority, and priesthood power. And I wanted to understand how a woman, who is not ordained, draws upon that power.

Women need to understand priesthood power just as much as men do.

Because of what I have learned, I wince when I hear a priesthood leader say, usually in a Relief Society meeting or women's conference of some kind, "I want to leave a blessing with each of you, particularly for those who don't have the priesthood in their home." As an unmarried but endowed woman, I do not have a priesthood bearer living in my home, but I do have access to priesthood power in my home. While being unmarried is a source of personal sadness and loneliness with which I grapple daily, it does not leave me (or any other endowed woman who lives alone but who understands what she has been endowed with) as defenseless and powerless as some apparently believe.

Further, I have learned for myself how tangible the power of priesthood keys is and how literally those keys authorize the flow of priesthood power to each of us. While serving in the Relief Society general presidency, another general officer and I traveled in a distant land with the Area President and his wife to a large city where the Church has many stakes—enough that one stake center could not accommodate all of the priesthood and auxiliary leaders assigned to attend the meetings in which we were participating. The Area President accompanied the other general officer to her meetings and asked me to go to a different chapel to teach the Relief Society and priesthood leaders assigned to that session. "Who will preside at the Relief Society training?" I asked. He indicated that one of the stake presidents there had been assigned to preside, and off I went.

When I arrived at my building, I found a stake center filled to capacity and many stake presidents waiting to greet and help me; but due to a miscommunication, no one had received the assignment to preside from the Area President. Because no stake president could appoint himself to preside, no one did.

As an unmarried but endowed woman, I do not have a priesthood bearer living in my home, but I do have access to priesthood power in my home.

The meeting that unfolded was a disaster. From the moment I stood to teach a three-hour session, it was clear to me (and I'm sure to everyone else) that I was on my own. I experienced the utter futility of attempting to serve without the power of a presiding authority. *Priesthood keys are real.* They unlock the power of God to all who serve under their direction. *Priesthood authority is real.* It enables men who are ordained and worthy to officiate in saving ordinances and to bless and heal those who have faith. *Priesthood power is real.* It is not some theological theory. It is the power of God Himself available to men and women alike who serve under the direction of those who have keys as well as to those who have been endowed in the house of the Lord.

I had an entirely different experience in Recife, Brazil. For meetings there, I had a translator who was highly skilled but anxious about doing side-by-side translation before a large audience of priesthood and auxiliary leaders. We were serving under the direction of Elder Claudio R. M. Costa, the Area President.

The meeting went well, and the translator did a beautiful job, with the interchange between the two of us at times feeling seamless. There were moments when it almost felt as though I was speaking Portuguese. After the meeting a stake president told me the rest of the story: "I wish you could have seen Elder Costa and the Area Seventy with him. They were on the edge of their seats, listening to every word you said and occasionally prompting the translator to make sure everything received a precise translation. I said to Elder Costa, 'I noticed that you listened carefully to what Sister Dew taught, even though you were the presiding authority.' 'Of course,' he said. 'She was assigned by the Brethren to bring us a message, and it was my responsibility to make sure we heard it exactly as she meant it.'" The Area Seventy then said to me, "Elder Costa told me my assignment was to pray for you and the translator throughout the meeting, so I did." Though I was serving under Elder Costa's direction, he in turn used his priesthood keys and authority to support and sustain me in my assignment. It was one of many experiences that have allowed me to see for myself the heavenly power that comes when righteous men and women support each other in their respective roles in the work of salvation.

Priesthood power is real. It is not some theological theory. It is the power of God Himself available to men and women alike who serve under the direction of those who have keys as well as to those who have been endowed in the house of the Lord.

That evening, I experienced firsthand what President Spencer W. Kimball was talking about when he said, "May the brotherhood of the priesthood and the sisterhood of the Relief Society be a blessing in the lives of all the members of this great Church, as we help each other along the path to perfection."[49]

For those concerned about the fact that LDS women are not ordained to the priesthood, the issue is in many respects one of priesthood keys. Those who hold keys ultimately govern the Church, and those individuals are men.

Why has the Lord organized His Church in this manner? I don't know. But followers of Christ have always been required to accept some things on faith. Unanswered questions are not unique in the annals of the Lord's Church. Only the Lord "knoweth all things."[50]

When all is said and done, as stated earlier, people of faith must *have* faith that the Lord has organized *His* Church according to *His* will, that *He* knows best what will lead all of us toward exaltation, that *He* is the one who determines those who will hold priesthood keys, and that *He* is the one who inspires them to use those keys according to *His* will.

While it is true that the mortals who hold keys are not perfect and do not always handle things flawlessly, our Father and His Son oversee all. In Their infinite wisdom and perfect knowledge and understanding, They have devised a plan and organized a Church designed to help us achieve our highest potential.

3. In the Temple, Both Men and Women Are "Endowed with the Same Power, Which by Definition Is Priesthood Power"

President Joseph Fielding Smith explained that "the blessings of the priesthood are not confined to men alone. These blessings are also poured out upon . . . all the faithful women of the Church. . . . The Lord offers to his daughters every spiritual gift and blessing that can be obtained by His sons."[51]

All of us, covenant men and women alike, receive the gift and power of the Holy Ghost. We may all speak and lead as directed by the Spirit, receive and understand the mysteries of the kingdom, and learn to open the heavens. We may *all* enjoy the ministering of and communion with angels (whom Joseph said *could not be restrained* from associating with women who were pure and innocent).[52] We may *all* take upon us the Lord's name, partake of the ordinances of the temple, receive the fulness of the gospel, become sons and daughters of Christ, and achieve exaltation in the celestial kingdom.[53] These spiritual blessings emanate from the Melchizedek Priesthood, which holds the "keys of all the spiritual blessings of the church."[54]

Priesthood power heals, blesses, protects, and inoculates all of the Father's righteous sons and daughters against the powers of darkness. It has the power to separate and safeguard us from the world, to subdue the adversary and help us surmount obstacles, to enlarge our physical and spiritual capacity and enable us to hear the voice of the Lord, to strengthen marriages and families and bind us to each other and to the Lord, and to allow us to triumph over mortality and come unto Him. These blessings may be received by every righteous son and daughter.[55]

Further, women who have received their endowment in the house of the Lord have additional privileges.

Endowed, covenant-keeping women have direct access to priesthood power for their own lives.

> *Endowed, covenant-keeping women have direct access to priesthood power for their own lives.*

What does it mean to have access to priesthood power for our own lives? It means that we can receive revelation, be blessed and aided by the ministering of angels, learn to part the veil that separates us from our Heavenly Father, be strengthened to resist temptation, be protected, and be enlightened and made smarter than we are—all without any mortal intermediary.

Eliza R. Snow said that Latter-day Saint women "have greater and higher privileges than any other females upon the face of the earth."[56] This is because the temple gives LDS women spiritual privileges no other women on earth may claim.

Men and women who are endowed in the house of the Lord have been given a gift of power, and they have been given a gift of knowledge to know how to access and use that power.

The temple is the only place on earth where we may receive the highest ordinances and greatest spiritual privileges and powers of mortality. It is *the ultimate institution of higher learning.* As important as traditional education is, the finest instruction in the world's finest universities pales when compared with what the Grand Schoolmaster teaches those who submit to the curriculum taught in His house.

Elder D. Todd Christofferson taught that the source of moral and spiritual power is God and that "our access to that power is through our covenants with Him. . . . In all the ordinances, especially those of the temple, we are endowed with power from on high."[57]

In the temple, we are promised that we may "grow up" in the Lord, receive a "fulness of the Holy Ghost," be armed with the power of the Lord, and have His name upon us, His glory round about us, and His angels given charge over us.[58]

Brigham Young explained that the endowment is "to receive all those ordinances in the house of the Lord, which are necessary for you, after you have departed this life, to enable you to walk back to the presence of the Father, passing the angels who stand as sentinels . . . and gain your eternal exaltation."[59]

Men and women who are endowed in the house of the Lord have been given a gift of power, and they have been given a gift of knowledge to know how to access and use that power.

President Young also said that "the priesthood is given to the people . . . and, when properly understood, they may actually unlock the treasury of the Lord, and receive to their fullest satisfaction."[60] Surely the "treasury of the Lord" includes the "wonders of eternity" and the "riches of eternity" that the Lord wishes to give His sons and daughters. Surely it includes the "mysteries of God" that are granted unto those who give Him heed and diligence.[61]

The temple is a step-by-step ascent toward God. Elder John A.

Widtsoe wrote that "the endowment is so richly symbolic that only a fool would attempt to describe it; it is so packed full of revelations to those who exercise their strength to seek and see, that no human words can explain or make clear the possibilities that reside in the temple service. The endowment which was given by revelation can best be understood by revelation."[62]

For each of us, men and women alike, our quest is not just to make and keep sacred covenants but to claim the promises and privileges that accompany the *highest* ordinances on earth.

> *For each of us, men and women alike, our quest is not just to make and keep sacred covenants but to claim the promises and privileges that accompany the* highest *ordinances on earth.*

LEARNING THE DOCTRINE OF THE PRIESTHOOD

Do I fully understand the doctrine of the priesthood? Of course not. I am simply an earnest student with average intellect. I know, however, that if we sincerely want to learn about the Lord and His ways, He will lead us along just as He did the Prophet Joseph—here a little, there a little.

The Prophet himself taught us this when he gave us insight into how much the Lord is willing to teach us: "God hath not revealed anything to Joseph, but what He will make known unto the Twelve, and *even the least Saint may know all things* as fast as he is able to bear them, for the day must come when no man need say to his neighbor, Know ye the Lord; for all shall know Him (who remain) from the least to the greatest."[63]

In that spirit, I share an example of being led along while pondering the issue of priesthood and its relationship to me as a woman. One day, I became curious about a passage in Doctrine and Covenants 84, which contains the oath and covenant of the priesthood. There we learn that those who are faithful and who "obtain" the Aaronic and Melchizedek Priesthood and then magnify their callings become "the sons of Moses and of Aaron and the seed of Abraham . . . and the elect of God."[64] These verses seem to apply solely to men.

Subsequent verses, however, say this: "And also all they who *receive* this priesthood *receive* me, saith the Lord; For he that *receiveth* my servants r*eceiveth* me; and he that *receiveth* me *receiveth* my Father; and he that *receiveth* my Father *receiveth* my Father's kingdom; therefore all that my Father hath shall be given unto him. And this is according to the oath and covenant which belongeth to the priesthood. Therefore, all those who *receive* the priesthood, *receive* this oath and covenant of my Father."[65]

The words *also all they* and the word *receive,* used no fewer than ten times in these verses, aroused my curiosity. The phrase *also all they* seems to refer to more than those who are ordained. And though we typically use *receive* to mean "to acquire something," *receive* can also mean "to believe" or "to accept as true."

Interestingly, this secondary definition of *receive* is used frequently in the scriptures by the Lord Himself. He began a revelation to Emma Smith by declaring that "all those who *receive* [accept] my gospel are sons and daughters in my kingdom."[66] On another occasion, the Savior lamented, "I came unto my own, and my own *received* [accepted] me not. . . . And as many as have *received* [accepted, believed in] me, to them have I given to become the sons of God."[67]

As I read verses such as these and pondered the secondary definition of *receive,* I found myself wondering if the transcendent promises of Doctrine and Covenants 84:35–40 might be available not only to those who receive the priesthood through ordination but also to those who receive its blessings by:

- *believing* that the priesthood is the power of God;
- *accepting* the manner in which the Lord has organized His kingdom;
- sustaining those who hold priesthood keys; and
- honoring priesthood power as the power of God.

In other words, could it be that the blessings of the oath and covenant of the priesthood are just as efficacious in the lives of endowed, covenant-keeping, believing women as they are for ordained men?

I do not share or declare these ponderings as doctrine but as reflections of someone engaged in the step-by-step, line-upon-line process of seeking to receive what the Lord has made available to us. At the very least, it seems clear from the scriptures that women have claim upon *all* blessings that emanate from priesthood keys, priesthood authority, and priesthood power.

We as women are not diminished by priesthood power, we are magnified by it. Endowed, covenant-keeping women have di-

We as women are not diminished by priesthood power, we are magnified by it. Righteous, endowed women have as much access to priesthood power and its blessings as do righteous, endowed, ordained men.

rect access to priesthood power for their own lives. The challenge and opportunity for each woman is to learn what that means and how to access that power.

4. Neither a Man nor a Woman May Receive the Highest Ordinances of the Priesthood or Be Exalted Alone

The ultimate aim of the Church and the Melchizedek Priesthood is to enable men and women to be exalted. Paul taught the Corinthians how this was to be done: "Neither is the man without the woman, neither the woman without the man, in the Lord."[68]

A *fulness of the priesthood,* and therefore the highest priesthood ordinances and the greatest priesthood power, are available only to a righteous man and woman together, just as exaltation is available only to a man and woman together—a couple who are "sealed in the new and everlasting covenant of marriage," who are true and faithful, and who qualify for a "fulness and a continuation of the seeds forever and ever. Then shall they be gods, because they have no end."[69] No one will be exalted alone.[70] Happily, there will be neither singles nor singles wards in the highest degree of the celestial kingdom![71]

Thus, in the sealing ordinance of the temple—an ordinance that elevates men and women and propels them along the path to exaltation—our Father has made clear His feelings about women, men, and marriage.

Our Father created men to need women and women to need men.

Elder John A. Widtsoe explained that "the Priesthood is for the benefit of all members of the Church. Men have no greater claim than women upon the blessings that issue from the Priesthood and accompany its possession. Woman does not hold the Priesthood, but she is a partaker of the blessings of the Priesthood. . . . This is made clear . . . in the Temple. . . . The ordinances of the Temple are distinctly of Priesthood character, yet women have access to *all* of them, and the highest blessings of the Temple are conferred only upon a man and his wife jointly."[72]

Elder Charles W. Penrose taught something similar: "When a woman is sealed to a man holding the Priesthood, she becomes one with him. . . . The glory and power and dominion that he will exercise when he has the fulness of the Priesthood and becomes 'a king and a priest unto God,' she will share with him."[73]

Our Father created men to need women and women to need men. In the Lord's kingdom, priesthood and parenthood are necessarily intertwined. The sealing ordinance makes this abundantly clear.

Elder Richard G. Scott declared that "in the Lord's plan, it takes two—a man and a woman—to form a whole. Indeed, a husband and wife are not two identical halves, but a wondrous, divinely determined combination of complementary capacities and characteristics."[74] Elder David A. Bednar added that "the unique combination of spiritual, physical, mental, and emotional capacities of both males and females was needed to enact the plan of happiness. . . . The man and the woman are intended to learn from, strengthen, bless, and complete each other."[75]

There is an interdependency between men and women that is essential not only for posterity and for lasting happiness but also for eternal life. Elder James E. Talmage addressed this issue when he taught that "women of the Church share the authority of the Priesthood with their husbands, *actual or prospective;* and therefore women . . . are not ordained to specific rank in the Priesthood. Nevertheless, there is no grade, rank, or phase of the temple endowment to which women are not eligible on an equality with men. . . . Within the House of the Lord the woman is the equal and the help-meet of the man. In the privileges and blessings of that holy place, the utterance of Paul is regarded as a scriptural decree in full force and effect. 'Neither is the man without the woman, neither the woman without the man, in the Lord.'"[76] Indeed, Peter spoke of husband and wife being "heirs together of the grace of life."[77]

On another occasion Elder Talmage added further clarification: "It is not given to woman to exercise the authority of the Priesthood independently; nevertheless, in the sacred endowments associated with the ordinances of the House of the Lord, woman shares with man the blessings of the Priesthood. . . . In the glorified state of the blessed hereafter, husband and wife will administer in their respective stations, seeing and understanding alike, and co-operating to the full in the government of their family kingdom. . . . Then shall woman reign by Divine right, a queen in the resplendent realm of her glorified state, even as exalted man shall stand, priest and king unto the Most High God. Mortal eye cannot see nor mind comprehend the beauty, glory, and majesty of a righteous woman made perfect in the celestial kingdom of God."[78]

Simply put, as President Harold B. Lee explained: "Pure womanhood plus priesthood means exaltation. But womanhood without priesthood, or priesthood without womanhood, doesn't spell exaltation."[79]

I know this is true. There isn't a day that I'm not acutely aware that as an unmarried woman, I am not yet complete.

Singleness does not equal exaltation.

A man and a woman, as designed by God, create a whole. President Gordon B. Hinckley went to the heart of the matter when he said, "There is no other arrangement that meets the divine purposes of the Almighty. Man and woman are His creations. Their duality is His design. Their complementary relationships and functions are fundamental to His purposes. One is incomplete without the other."[80]

Elder Bruce C. Hafen taught that when a man and woman come together in righteousness, "spouses need not perform the same functions to be equal. The woman's innate spiritual instincts are like a moral magnet, pointing toward spiritual north—except when that magnet's particles are scrambled out of order. The man's presiding gift is the priesthood—except when he is not living the principles of righteousness. If the husband and the wife are wise, their counseling will be reciprocal: he will listen to the promptings of her inner spiritual compass just as she will listen to his righteous counsel."[81]

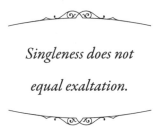

Singleness does not equal exaltation.

Elder Hafen recounted an episode in the biography of Elder Neal A. Maxwell illustrating this principle: "When Elder Maxwell learned in 1996 that he had leukemia, the diagnosis was discouraging. He had worked for years on making himself 'willing to submit' (Mosiah 3:19) to the Lord's will. If it was time to face death, he didn't want to shrink from drinking his bitter cup. But his wife, Colleen, thought he was too willing to yield. With loving directness, she said that Christ Himself earnestly pleaded first, 'If it be possible, let this cup pass from me.' Only then did He submit Himself, saying, 'Nevertheless not as I will, but as thou wilt' (Matthew 26:39). Elder Maxwell saw his wife's doctrinal insight and agreed. As a result, they pleaded together that his life might be spared. Motivated by their determination, Elder Maxwell's doctor found a new medical treatment that prolonged his life for several years."[82]

Elder John A. Widtsoe offered this insight: "Modern revelation sets forth the high destiny of those who are sealed for everlasting companionship. They will be given opportunity for a greater use of their powers. That means progress. They will attain more readily to their place in the presence of the Lord; they will increase more readily in every divine power; they will approach more nearly to the likeness of God; they will more completely realize their divine destiny."[83]

Elder Bruce R. McConkie taught that there is much to learn in this regard from our first parents: "As [Adam and Eve] have gone on to exaltation and sit upon their thrones in glorious immortality, so may all, both male and female, who walk as they walked. As there are no words to extol the greatness of the Ancient of Days . . . , so there is no language that can do credit to our glorious mother Eve."[84]

Neither men nor women have an edge over the other when it comes to qualifying for exaltation. Very simply, the highest ordinances of the house of the Lord, and ultimately eternal life, are available only to a man and woman together.

FAITH IN GOD AND IN HIS POWER

There are many things about the priesthood and the division of responsibilities between men and women that I don't yet understand. This does not concern me, however, because wrestling with spiritual questions is a fundamental element of a religious life. It is an exercise that not only increases knowledge but strengthens faith.

Furthermore, the things I don't yet understand do not negate what I do know. I know that Joseph Smith was a prophet, foreordained by the Lord to be *the* Prophet of this dispensation, the one through whom the Lord restored His gospel and His priesthood.

Wrestling with spiritual questions is a fundamental element of a religious life. It is an exercise that not only increases knowledge but strengthens faith.

I know that we have a living prophet and living Apostles today who hold all priesthood keys and who receive revelation for the Church. I know that the priesthood has been restored to the earth for the benefit and blessing of men and women alike, and that priesthood keys literally unlock God's authority and power in behalf of all of us. And I know that endowed, covenant-keeping men and women have access to priesthood power for their own lives.

In a sobering passage of scripture, the Lord taught Joseph Smith that there will be many who are consigned to the telestial or terrestrial kingdoms, to enjoy what they were "willing to receive, because they were not willing to enjoy that which they might have received. For what doth it profit a man if a gift is bestowed upon him, and he receive not the gift? Behold, he rejoices not in that which is given unto him, neither rejoices in him who is the giver of the gift."[85]

How ironic it is that some are annoyed by our mortal perspectives of the priesthood and how the Lord has chosen to disperse it throughout the Church when actually priesthood power and *all* of its blessings are here to help, strengthen, enlighten, protect, and redeem *everyone* who believes and seeks. How tragic it will be if that sense of annoyance leads some to overlook the tremendous gifts that can be ours if we will but receive and learn how to access them. What we understand and how we feel about the priesthood is central to our testimony of the restored gospel.[86]

So, back to an earlier question: What do Latter-day Saint women get?

As baptized, endowed daughters of God, we have the privilege of:

• receiving the gift and power of the Holy Ghost;

• receiving personal revelation;

• being endowed in the temple with godly power and with the knowledge to access that power;

• leading and teaching by the Spirit;

• having angels as our associates;

- receiving spiritual gifts—including charity, spiritual intuition, and moral courage, which are found in women in abundance;

- receiving all of the blessings of the Atonement;

- entering the new and everlasting covenant of marriage;

- bearing and rearing children and becoming partners with the Almighty in the progression of His children; and

- most important, we have the opportunity to receive eternal life. As Paul taught the Romans: We are "heirs of God, and joint-heirs with Christ; if so be that we suffer with him, that we may be also glorified together."[87]

What do Mormon women get? Potentially, we get everything.

Chapter 7

GOD RESERVED THE HIGH PRIVILEGE OF MOTHERHOOD FOR WOMEN

A few years back, I boarded a plane in Salt Lake City and found myself seated next to a woman who identified herself as a member of the Church and then proceeded to tell me about an encounter she had just had in the airport's VIP lounge with a pair of famous rappers who were passing through Salt Lake City on their way from L.A. to the East Coast. Why a couple of rappers struck up a conversation with a strait-laced Mormon mom is a mystery, but they did. The more they talked, the louder and more brazen their claims about their fame became. When they boasted that they had gotten more teenagers hooked on sex and drugs than anyone else in the music business, this woman had had enough. "At first, I tried to be polite," she said. "But the longer they bragged about how famous they were and how many teenagers they had polluted and destroyed, the madder I became. Finally, my Mother Bear instincts got the best of me and I said to them, 'Gentlemen, you've been open with me, so I assume you expect the same in return. Before you go any further, you need to know that I've spent my entire life trying to protect youth from people like you.'"

One of a mother's most instinctive inclinations is to safeguard her children—and she will willingly forego her own safety, comfort, health, and even reputation to do so. The "Mother Bear" syndrome is real; in fact, it is divine. Our Father has entrusted His daughters with His children. He has asked us not only to love them but to help lead them safely back home through this spook alley we call mortality.[1]

One Sunday while I was teaching a Relief Society lesson on the distractions that plague women today, an adorable young mother, pregnant with her fourth, raised her hand and shared a recent experience: "I attended a banquet the other night with my husband," she said, "and we were seated next to the guests of honor—a husband and wife whose accomplishments were legendary. Partway through the dinner, the man being honored turned to me and asked, 'What do *you* do?' There I was, eight months pregnant. I'm sorry to admit that in that moment I felt reluctant to say that I was a stay-at-home mom. But I finally told him that taking care of my husband and our three children, with the fourth on the way, was more than a full-time job. 'Oh,' he responded, and then turned to find someone more interesting to talk to. All night I was bothered about that conversation—not as much with his response as with how his question made me feel about being a mother. I love being a mother! But for a few moments, I was embarrassed that that was all I had to say for myself."

> *Our Father has entrusted His daughters with His children. He has asked us not only to love them but to help lead them safely back home through this spook alley we call mortality.*

Heads nodded in agreement around the Relief Society room. Clearly others related to her experience. I suggested that the next time someone asks that question—because someone will—she consider responding, "I'm shepherding four children along the path to exaltation. How about you?"

The reality is that the effectiveness of the plan of salvation in the lives of God's children hangs to a large degree on the character; the never-ending, bone-wearying work; and the faith of righteous mothers. The world doesn't recognize this, but it's true.

For those with the lenses of eternal life, could anything be more important than helping to shepherd our Father's sons and daughters along the path that leads ultimately to exaltation? Prophets, seers, and revelators have repeatedly answered this question, as did Elder Jeffrey R. Holland when he told women that "there is nothing more important in this world than participating so directly in the work and glory of God, in bringing to pass the mortality and earthly life of His daughters and sons, so that immortality and eternal life can come in those celestial realms on high."[2]

> *For those with the lenses of eternal life, could anything be more important than helping to shepherd our Father's sons and daughters along the path that leads ultimately to exaltation?*

President Heber J. Grant was explicit about the extent of a mother's impact, declaring that "the mother in the family far more than the father is the one who instills into the hearts of the children a testimony, and love of the gospel—and wherever you find a woman who is devoted to this work, almost without exception you will find that her children are devoted to it. She shapes their lives more than the father."[3] Indeed, in the final moments of His anguish, the Savior signaled His reverence for mothers and motherhood when He looked down from the cross, saw and singled out His mother, and instructed John, "Behold thy mother."[4]

THE DOCTRINE OF MOTHERHOOD

Prophets have taught the doctrine of motherhood again and again. And *it is* doctrine. The doctrine of motherhood has less to do with earthly child-bearing—though it certainly includes and is epitomized by bearing children—than it does with eternal privileges, responsibilities, and endowments. Motherhood in its doctrinal sense can only fully be exercised upon principles of righteousness—much the same as priesthood authority[5]—and can be understood and exercised by all righteous women, not just those who have the privilege of bearing children in this life.

Motherhood is a doctrine about which we must be clear if we hope to stand steadfast and immovable regarding the issues that swirl around the female gender and the family.

Elder Dallin H. Oaks taught: "Maleness and femaleness, marriage, and the bearing and nurturing of children are all essential to the great plan of happiness. . . . To the first man and woman on earth, the Lord said, 'Be fruitful, and multiply' (Moses 2:28; see also Gen. 1:28; Abr. 4:28). This commandment was first in sequence and first in importance."[6]

The doctrine of motherhood has less to do with earthly child-bearing—though it certainly includes and is epitomized by bearing children—than it does with eternal privileges, responsibilities, and endowments.

Precisely because the bearing of children is vital to God's plan for His children, and nurturing those children in the admonition of the Lord is fundamental to giving His children their greatest chance of ultimate success, Satan has declared war on motherhood and on the family. He knows that those who rock the cradle are in the best possible position to rock his diabolical earthly empire. He knows that none of us can progress without receiving bodies and experiencing our mortal estate. This knowledge must be piercing for him, as he has lost his chance for a body forever.

President Spencer W. Kimball taught that it is no accident that Heavenly Father's plan for His sons and daughters calls for children to be born to a man and woman: "This is a program carefully planned. The Lord could have provided some other way, but how could parents love and nurture their children in such a case? The bodies of men and women were created differently so they complemented each other, so that the union of the two would bring a conception which would bring a living soul into the world. . . . The whole program was intelligently organized to bring children into the world with love and filial interdependence. Had the superficial ideas of many mortals of today prevailed, the world, the human race, and all proper things would long ago have come to an end."[7]

In another setting, President Kimball added, "The Lord holds motherhood and mothers sacred and in the highest esteem. . . . Life cannot go on if women cease to bear children. Mortal life is a privilege and a necessary step in eternal progression. Mother Eve understood that. You must also understand it."[8]

Not only do we *not* have a worldwide population explosion, claimed for so long by scientific elites, but the list of countries whose population growth has sunk below the replacement rate is growing at an alarming rate. And the United States has now joined that club.

Jonathan V. Last, author of *What to Expect When No One's Expecting: America's Coming Demographic Disaster,* explained how serious the situation is: "For more than three decades, Chinese women have been subjected to their country's brutal one-child policy. Those who try to have more children have been subjected to fines and forced abortions. Their houses have been razed and their husbands fired from their jobs. As a result, Chinese women have a fertility rate of 1.54. Here in America, white, college-educated women—a good proxy for the middle class—have a fertility rate of 1.6. America has its very own one-child policy. And we have chosen it for ourselves. Forget the debt ceiling. Forget the fiscal cliff, the sequestration cliff and the entitlement cliff. Those are all just symptoms. What America really faces is a demographic cliff."[9]

It doesn't take a mathematician to calculate the impact on society of a population that won't replace itself. Even more serious is the attempted threat to our Heavenly Father's plan for His children. Mortal life is a prerequisite for eternal life.

Let's be clear: Lucifer is utterly anti-progression. He can never dig himself out of the pit he's in. His only satisfaction, if it can be called that, is to entice others to join him there—to prevent others from going places he will never go and to persuade as many as possible to abuse the body he will never have.

But Satan is never satisfied. He cannot corrupt enough people to satiate his evil nature, because evil never tires of evil. His is the ultimate misery-loves-company attitude. He is the most evil of evil spirits, and that's all he will ever be. Imagine the tortured state in which he exists: he fell from heaven, has become "miserable forever," and seeks constantly the "misery of all mankind."[10] Because he doesn't have a body, his misery is confined to his mind. He knows he'll never have a body, never progress, never be freed from his current condition, never be anything more than what he currently is.

Mortal life is a prerequisite for eternal life.

The adversary clearly understands that mothers who are willing to bear children and give them the gift and privilege of receiving a body, and particularly righteous mothers who will not only bear children but bear *with* them while leading them along a faithful path, are a vital key to our Father's plan for *His* children.

THE MAGNITUDE OF MOTHERHOOD

Motherhood is divine, eternal, and core to the nature of every woman.

When we understand the magnitude of motherhood, it becomes clear why prophets have been so protective of woman's most sacred and divinely appointed role. Here in mortality we tend to equate motherhood solely with maternity, but in the Lord's language the word *mother* has layers of meaning. Of all the words or titles they could have chosen to define her role and her essence, both God the Father and Adam called Eve "the mother of all living," and they did so before she ever bore a child. "And Adam called his wife's name Eve, because she was the mother of all living; for thus have I, the Lord God, called the first of all women, which are many."[11]

As President Hugh B. Brown taught, "Jesus honored womanhood when he came to this earth as a little child through the sacred and glorious agency of motherhood; thus motherhood became akin to Godhood."[12]

Here in mortality we tend to equate motherhood solely with maternity, but in the Lord's language the word mother *has layers of meaning. Of all the words or titles they could have chosen to define her role and her essence, both God the Father and Adam called Eve "the mother of all living," and they did so before she ever bore a child.*

And seven decades ago, the First Presidency called motherhood "the highest, holiest service . . . assumed by mankind."[13]

The Lord does nothing with a short-range view. Everything He does is for forever. Thus, like Eve, our motherhood began before we were born. Just as worthy men were foreordained to hold the priesthood in mortality,[14] righteous women were endowed premortally with the high privilege and responsibility of motherhood.[15]

Motherhood is more than bearing children, though it is certainly that. It is the essence of who we are as women.

Motherhood defines our very identity, our divine stature and nature, and the unique traits, talents, and tendencies with which our Father endowed us.

President Gordon B. Hinckley stated that "God planted within women something divine."[16] That something is the gift of, and the gifts associated with, motherhood. Speaking to women, Elder Matthew Cowley of the Quorum of the Twelve taught that "you belong to the great sorority of saviorhood. . . . Men are different, men have to have something given to them [in mortality] to make them saviors of men, but not mothers, not women. You are born with an inherent right, an inherent authority, to be the saviors of human souls. You are the co-creators with God of his children. Therefore, it is expected of you by a right divine that you're the saviors and the regenerating force in the lives of God's children here upon the earth."[17]

President David O. McKay was explicit when he stated that motherhood was "the noblest office or calling in the world. She who can paint a masterpiece or write a book that will influence millions deserves the admiration and the plaudits of mankind; but she who rears successfully a family of healthy, beautiful sons and daughters, whose influence will be felt through generations to come, whose immortal souls will exert an influence throughout the ages long after paintings shall have faded, and books and statues shall have decayed or shall have been destroyed, deserves the highest honor that man can give, and the choicest blessings of God. In her high duty and service to humanity, endowing with immortality eternal spirits, she is co-partner with the Creator himself."[18]

> *Motherhood is more than bearing children, though it is certainly that. It is the essence of who we are as women.*

Or, as Elder Russell M. Nelson clarified, "When a mother bears and cares for a child, she not only helps the earth answer the end of its creation, but she glorifies God!"[19]

Motherhood is not what was left over after our Father blessed His sons with the privilege of priesthood ordination. It was *the most ennobling endowment* He could give His daughters, a sacred trust that gave women the guiding role in partnering with our Father in the act of creation and then in helping His children keep their second estate.

Illustrating this fact, Elder John A. Widtsoe declared that "no man who understands the gospel believes that he is greater than his wife, or more beloved of the Lord, because he holds the Priesthood. . . . It is a protection to the woman who, because of her motherhood, is under a large physical and spiritual obligation. *Motherhood is an eternal part of Priesthood.*"[20]

President J. Reuben Clark Jr. added that motherhood is "as divinely called, as eternally important in its place as the Priesthood itself."[21] And President Boyd K. Packer taught that "the limitation of priesthood responsibilities to men is a tribute to the incomparable place of women in the plan of salvation. . . . Men and women have complementary, not competing, responsibilities. There is difference but not inequity. . . . In the woman's part, she is not equal to man; she is superior! She can do that which he can never do; not in all eternity can he do it."[22]

> *Motherhood is not what was left over after our Father blessed His sons with the privilege of priesthood ordination. It was the most ennobling endowment He could give His daughters, a sacred trust that gave women the guiding role in partnering with our Father in the act of creation and then in helping His children keep their second estate.*

Eve came to mother an entire world. And every woman who bears children follows in her footsteps by bringing life to earth. No wonder President Brigham Young declared that "mothers are the machinery that give zest to the whole man, and guide the destinies and lives of men upon the earth."[23] And President Hugh B. Brown stated, "You women exert the first and most lasting influence on your child when you co-operate with God in building its body. As you cradle it in your arms, nourish and nurture it by your love and sacrifice, as you stimulate its intellect, its ambition, strengthen its spiritual and moral fiber, you are intimately co-operating with your Heavenly Father."[24]

Women have been entrusted with the *single most crucial* assignment related to our Father's children fulfilling their mission on earth—to keep our "second estate" so that "glory [can be] added upon [our] heads for ever and ever."[25]

President Boyd K. Packer explained, "To women is given a most supernal part of the plan of redemption." Then, speaking directly to the women of the Church, President Packer counseled: "Foster in yourself and in your daughters the exalted role of the woman, the incomparable gift of creation that attends motherhood. The man was given to provide and protect; the woman was given to make it all worthwhile."[26]

I have friends, a husband and wife, who have served widely in the Church and at the same time raised a large and close-knit family. The husband has also enjoyed sustained professional success. One day I asked how they had managed it all. "One day early in our marriage the light clicked on for me," he explained. "It happened after we had been to an event sponsored by my work. One person after another complimented my wife on supporting me in my career. As we drove home, it dawned on me that actually *I was the one* doing the supporting. I went to work every day to make it possible for her to stay home with our children and focus without distraction on *the most important work* we as a couple would ever do—and that was raise our children to love the Lord."

President Packer reinforced the truth of this insight when he declared that "the greatest teaching in the Church is done by mothers."[27]

THE TENDER REALITIES OF MOTHERHOOD

There is no question about how our Father feels about His daughters, whom He has charged with the principal care of His children. Nevertheless, at times and in some circumstances, the words *mother* and *motherhood* have divided rather than united us. The subject of motherhood is a tender one, as it evokes some of our greatest joys and heartaches. This has been so from the very beginning. Eve was "glad" after the Fall, realizing she otherwise "never should have had seed."[28] So Mother Eve began the human race with gladness, wanting children, willing to take the joy along with whatever pain would come.

And there *was* pain. Imagine her anguish over Cain and her heartache about Abel. Some women experience pain because of the children they have borne. "Sometimes the decision of a child or a grandchild will break your heart," said Elder Jeffrey R. Holland. "Even that beloved and wonderfully successful parent President Joseph F. Smith pled, 'Oh! God, let me not lose my own.' That is every parent's cry. . . . But no one has failed who keeps trying and keeps praying. You have every right to receive encouragement and to know in the end your children will call your name blessed, just like those generations of foremothers before you who hoped your same hopes and felt your same fears."[29]

The Lord's timetable for each of us does not negate or somehow change or cancel out our very nature. Some must find other ways to mother. All around us are those who need to be loved and led, nurtured and mentored. In other words, the spiritual rewards and responsibilities of mothering are available to all.

Other women feel pain because they are deprived of bearing children in mortality. About this Elder John A. Widtsoe was explicit: "Women who through no fault of their own cannot exercise the gift of motherhood directly, may so do vicariously."[30] And Elder Melvin J. Ballard stated, "God bless those mothers who are not yet permitted through no fault of their own to be mothers in very deed, but who are nevertheless mothers at heart."[31]

At the funeral services for Eliza R. Snow, a woman who never bore a child in mortality, Elder John W. Taylor of the Quorum of the Twelve Apostles eulogized her in this way: "[Though the] deceased was deprived of bearing children, she is entitled to be called Mother among this people. . . . She has passed through trials and tribulations. She has made us joyful by her poetical effusions; we have sorrowed when she sorrowed, and we have rejoiced when she rejoiced. I pray that all who have seen her good works may endeavor to emulate them. . . . I pray . . . that whenever we think of Eliza R. Snow Smith, we will not think of her as 'Aunt Eliza' in the future, but that we may in truth and righteousness call her Mother."[32]

For reasons known to the Lord, some women are required to wait to have children. This delay and disappointment is not easy for any righteous woman. But the Lord's timetable for each of us does not negate or somehow change or cancel out our very nature. Some must find other ways to mother. All around us are those who need to be loved and led, nurtured and mentored. In other words, the spiritual rewards and responsibilities of mothering are available to all.

EVE SET THE PATTERN

Once again, Eve set the pattern. In addition to bearing children, she mothered all of mankind when she made *the* most courageous decision any woman has ever made and with Adam opened the way for us to progress. She set an example of womanhood for men to respect and women to follow, modeling the characteristics that the women of God have everlastingly demonstrated: heroic faith, a keen sensitivity to the Spirit, an abhorrence of evil, and complete selflessness. Like the Savior, "who for the joy that was set before him endured the cross,"[33] Eve, for the joy of helping initiate the human family, endured the Fall. She loved us enough to help lead us.

As daughters of our Heavenly Father, and as daughters of Eve, we are all mothers and we have always been mothers. And we each have the responsibility and the privilege to love and to help lead the rising generation and to model righteous womanhood. Regardless of our circumstances, we are each in a position to help enrich, protect, and guard the family, the home, and those within our sphere of influence.

As daughters of our Heavenly Father, and as daughters of Eve, we are all mothers and we have always been mothers.

President Henry B. Eyring has spoken of his wife's constant awareness of others: "My family's bishop said to me years ago, with a smile, 'Why is it that when I go to someone in the ward in need, your wife always seems to have been there ahead of me?'" President Eyring continued, elaborating on the unique nurturing gifts of women: "Every bishop and branch president with any experience at all has felt the gentle prod of inspired example from the sisters of the Relief Society. They help us remember that for all, both women and men, there will be no salvation without compassionate service."[34]

Compassion, courage, encouragement, and faith are the hallmarks of righteous mothers. The Apostle Paul praised Timothy's "unfeigned faith," attributing it to the influence of his grandmother Lois and his mother, Eunice.[35]

When I was growing up, it was not uncommon for Mother to wake me in the middle of the night with the words, "Sheri, take your pillow and go downstairs." I knew what that meant. We lived in a strip of the U.S. known as tornado alley, and in the spring there were often twisters nearby. My immediate reaction was always fear. But I learned to listen for Mom to say, "Everything will be okay," and I would calm down. If she believed, I believed.

Later, as I grew older and began to enter musical competitions and participate on athletic teams, before big games or performances, I would listen for Mother to say, "You can do it. You'll be great."

Today, decades later, when the pressures of life seem overwhelming or downright scary, I call Mother and listen for her to say, "Everything will be okay." I've learned that President Boyd K. Packer's statement is true, that "there are few things more powerful than the faithful prayers of a righteous mother."[36] The influence of a mother's prayers not only spans decades but can reach into the eternities.

When mothers are strong, their children—regardless of challenges— tend to be strong. When they are resilient and filled with faith, their children tend to be also. When they're virtuous, their children are more likely to be virtuous and to value virtue.

Academy Award–winning film director Kieth Merrill explains that there is a reason we find few strong mothers in movies today: "If you're a screenwriter and understand the essence of drama and you want to plunge your characters into conflict and keep them there, then you probably need to 'lose the mom.' Mothers go missing in movies because leaving them in the lives of characters in crisis makes sustaining conflict difficult. Mothers listen and understand, solve problems and resolve conflicts. They are selfless and love without conditions. You want to stir up a heap of trouble and make it believable? Better keep Mom out of it."[37]

Lucy Mack Smith, mother of the Prophet Joseph, showed how life-changing a mother's influence and a mother's prayers can be. Long before her son had the experience in the Sacred Grove that commenced the Restoration, she earnestly sought to find the original gospel preached by the Savior. After attending one of many religious revivals, she wrote: "I went in expectation of obtaining that which alone could satisfy my soul—the bread of eternal life. When the minister commenced, I fixed my mind with breathless attention upon the spirit and matter of the discourse, but all was emptiness, vanity, vexation of spirit, and fell upon my heart like the chill, untimely blast upon the starting ear ripening in a summer sea. . . . I was almost in total despair, and with a grieved and troubled spirit I returned home, saying in my heart, there is not on earth the religion which I seek. I must again turn to my Bible, take Jesus and his disciples for an example."

"Mothers go missing in movies because leaving them in the lives of characters in crisis makes sustaining conflict difficult."

—KIETH MERRILL

When Lucy later nearly died of tuberculosis, she wrote, "I covenanted with God that if he would let me live, I would endeavor to get that religion that would enable me to serve him right, whether it was in the Bible or wherever it might be found, even if it was to be obtained from heaven by prayer and faith."[38]

Joseph Smith's mother was an earnest student of the scriptures and a believing woman. Surely her prayers of faith and years of seeking to find the Lord's Church created an environment in which the young Joseph Smith could develop spiritually—a home in which the scriptures and belief in God were central. Her influence has reached into the eternities.

OUR MOTHER IN HEAVEN

There are those who feel that it's difficult to fully appreciate or understand our calling as mothers when we know so little about our Mother in Heaven.

Zina Diantha Huntington, who would later serve as the third general president of the Relief Society, was eighteen when she lost her mother under difficult circumstances in Nauvoo. She asked the Prophet Joseph Smith if she would know her mother in the next world. "Certainly you will," he responded. "More than that, you will meet and become acquainted with your eternal Mother, the wife of your Father in Heaven." Having never contemplated such a thing, she questioned, "And have I, then, a Mother in Heaven?" to which the Prophet is said to have responded, "You assuredly have. How could a Father claim His title unless there were also a Mother to share that parenthood?" The record in which this account is written indicates that "it was about this time that Sister [Eliza R.] Snow learned the same glorious truth from the same inspired lips, and at once she was moved to express her own great joy and gratitude in the moving words of the hymn, 'O My Father.'"[39]

It is true that throughout this dispensation, very little has been revealed or taught about this matter, though "The Family: A Proclamation to the World" declares that "all human beings—male and female—are created in the image of God. Each is a beloved spirit son or daughter of *heavenly parents,* and, as such, each has a divine nature and destiny."[40] Eliza's text in "O My Father" contains what is perhaps the most familiar reference to our Heavenly Mother:

> *In the heav'ns are parents single?*
> *No, the thought makes reason stare!*

Truth is reason; truth eternal
Tells me I've a mother there.[41]

One could conjecture about why our Father in Heaven has elected not to reveal much about our Mother in Heaven. But the truth is that we don't know. I feel a quiet peace about the matter and an assurance that in the due time of the Lord, it will become clear why our Father has protected Her identity.

LOVING AND LEADING

Mothering isn't easy. Most mothers struggle to feel that they're having much impact or doing a good job. Elder Holland spoke of a young mother who shared that her anxieties tended to come in three ways: "One was that whenever she heard talks on LDS motherhood, she worried because she felt she didn't measure up or somehow wasn't going to be equal to the task," he related. "Secondly, she felt like the world expected her to teach her children reading, writing, interior design, Latin, calculus, and the Internet—all before her baby said something terribly ordinary, like 'goo goo.' Thirdly, she often felt people were sometimes patronizing, . . . because the advice she got or even the compliments she received seemed to reflect nothing of the mental investment, the spiritual and emotional exertion, the long-night, long-day, stretched-to-the-limit demands that sometimes are required in trying to be and wanting to be the mother God hopes she will be. But one thing, she said, keeps her going: 'Through the thick and the thin of this, and

Every time we build the faith or reinforce the nobility of a young woman or young man, every time we love or lead anyone even one step along the path, we are true to our endowment, calling, and inherent nature as mothers.

through the occasional tears of it all, *I know deep down inside I am doing God's work.'"*[42]

Every time we build the faith or reinforce the nobility of a young woman or young man, every time we love or lead anyone even one step along the path, we are true to our endowment, calling, and inherent nature as mothers. Nonetheless, there are some who chafe at the notion that motherhood is a woman's highest, holiest calling, or who reject any parallel treatment of priesthood and motherhood, or who just don't want to be confined to the home. I overheard one LDS woman recently express what no doubt others feel: "I don't want to be *just* a mother. I want to do something big in the world, something important."

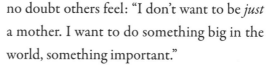

For every woman, the challenge is one of discerning the Lord's will for her and then following the promptings of the Spirit. None of our divine errands are exactly the same.

Admittedly, it has been difficult for me to understand that point of view, as I've spent my adult life praying for the privilege of motherhood. Yet in our day, some women consciously choose not to have children. I can't help but wonder if tugging against motherhood on this side of the veil could prove awkward when we arrive on the other side. I find myself imagining a conversation with our Father that might go something like this: "Let me be sure I'm clear," He might begin. "I gave you, my daughter, the highest privilege of which I know, the privilege of participating in the process of creation, of creating new life. And because your role is so central to my plan for my children, I gave my sons the assignment and the power to provide for you, to protect you, and to make sure you had what you needed so that you could focus on helping my children have every opportunity to return to live with me. But you wanted something else? You preferred not to be in an eternal partnership with me, even God?"

This is not to suggest that motherhood is the only meaningful way women can or should contribute in this world. For every woman, the challenge is one of discerning the Lord's will *for her* and then following the promptings of the Spirit. None of our divine errands are exactly the same.

Elder Quentin L. Cook acknowledged that decisions women make regarding children and other life activities are personal and then suggested two principles all should keep in mind: "First, no woman should ever feel the need to apologize or feel that her contribution is less significant because she is devoting her primary efforts to raising and nurturing children. Nothing could be more significant in our Father in Heaven's plan. Second, we should all be careful not to be judgmental or assume that sisters are less valiant if the decision is made to work outside the home. We rarely understand or fully appreciate people's circumstances. Husbands and wives should prayerfully counsel together, understanding they are accountable to God for their decisions."[43]

In the premortal world, when our Father described our role, I wonder if we didn't stand in wide-eyed wonder that He would bless us with a sacred trust so central to His plan and that He would endow us with gifts so vital to the loving and leading of His children.

I repeat: The issues that swirl around women are complicated and emotional. When all is said and done, however, no woman who understands the gospel would be inclined to say or feel, "I am *just* a mother." Mothers heal the souls of men. They not only give life—they breathe life into all who come under their mothering influence.

"Other institutions in society may falter and even fail," President Spencer W. Kimball warned, "but the righteous woman can help to save the home, which may be the last and only sanctuary some mortals know in the midst of storm and strife."[44]

Motherhood is a sacred trust because mothers literally shape the destiny of mankind. This is not hyperbole. The future of mankind is in the hands of mothers. The oft-quoted proverb, "Train up a child in the way he should go: and when he is old, he will not depart from it,"[45] shines a light on the power of righteous parenting. It just may be that mothers do more to train the next generation than all the other teachers of children put together.

As mothers in Israel, we *are* the Lord's secret weapon. Our influence comes from a divine endowment that has been in place from the beginning. In the premortal world, when our Father described our role, I wonder if we didn't stand in wide-eyed wonder that He would bless us with a sacred trust so central to His plan and that He would endow us with gifts so vital to the loving and leading of His children. I wonder if we shouted for joy[46] at least in part because of the ennobling stature He gave us in His kingdom.

The day may soon come when Latter-day Saint women are among the relatively few women on earth who find nobility and divinity in motherhood. In fact, a woman by the name of Lillie Freeze recorded that Joseph Smith said the "time would come when none but the women of the Latter-day Saints would be willing to bear children."[47]

So be it. For *mother* is the word that will define a righteous woman made perfect in the highest degree of the celestial kingdom, a woman who has qualified for eternal increase in posterity, wisdom, joy, and influence.

Chapter 8

CONVERTED WOMEN CAN CHANGE THE WORLD

I recently had the privilege of attending Relief Society at the Missionary Training Center in Provo, Utah. I say *privilege* because it is always an exquisite spiritual experience to be in the presence of full-time missionaries. But this most recent experience was unique. There were more sisters at the MTC than ever before, so in sheer volume that meeting was distinctive. And the exuberance of these youthful sister missionaries was electrifying. Then, before the meeting began, the large audience of missionaries stood and sang "As Sisters in Zion." At least, I thought it was "As Sisters in Zion." The melody by Janice Kapp Perry was the same, but the text was different.

I've sung that penetrating hymn in dozens of countries and languages and in literally thousands of congregations of sisters, and I've been moved by it again and again. But this meeting was different. Sister Perry had re-titled the hymn "The Sisters of Zion" and written new words especially for sister missionaries:

The sisters of Zion are called to God's labor,
We willingly serve Him with spirit and might!
We go to the nations with truth everlasting,
We teach of the Savior, our Lord Jesus Christ.

We thank thee, O God, for a prophet to guide us,
We trust in his words and our purpose is clear.
The angels of heaven are walking beside us,
We'll share our glad message with all who will hear.

We go forth enlisted with Helaman's Army,
In numbers far greater than ever before.
With power and spirit we'll faithfully witness
The heavens have spoken, and truth is restored![1]

As we sang these words in what was a deeply moving experience, I looked out over the vast audience of young-adult-age women who have stepped forward to serve the Lord full-time. The presence of the Spirit was palpable. But as we sang, I couldn't help but feel that Sister Perry's inspired new lyrics were just as relevant for all the women of the Church.

We *have all* been called to labor, to serve the Lord with spirit and might.

Nearly seven million strong, we are scattered throughout the nations of the earth, positioned to share our testimonies of Jesus Christ by what we say and do.

We have a prophet to guide us and heaven to help us.

We form a battalion in the army of the Lord greater than ever before.

With access to the power of God, we may each witness that the heavens are open and that truth has been restored.

These lyrics highlight a simple but profoundly significant truth: Converted women can change the world.

TRUTHS THAT SHOULD INTEREST US

There are fundamental truths that ought to interest every one of us living in the latter part of the latter days.

First, the Savior really is going to come again. And though we don't know the hour or the day of that remarkable event, we do know that the time is getting closer, not further away. We also know that "something is going to be asked of this dispensation that's never been asked before," as Elder Jeffrey R. Holland explained. "Those of this dispensation must be ready to present the Church of the Lamb, to the Lamb, and when that happens we must be looking and acting like His Church."[2]

Second, we really are going to live forever. Where we live, how we live, and with whom we live is largely up to us. In large measure, we control our eternal destiny. Because our Father gave us agency, we have the freedom to choose how to spend our time, how to behave, how to treat others, what to care about, what to devote ourselves to, and what to learn in this life. It is up to us. And how we choose is key to how we will live forever.

The Savior really is going to come again. And though we don't know the hour or the day of that remarkable event, we do know that the time is getting closer, not further away.

Third, there isn't much we will take with us when we leave here. My father passed away last year. He spent his life, like his father and grandfather before him, building and operating a large agricultural operation in the Midwest. He loved everything about farming. But when he passed away, that farming operation—all the land, the machinery, the farmsteads, everything—became insignificant to his eternal life. As it will be for each of us, he was able to take with him the covenants he had made, the sum total of the person he had become in terms of character and integrity and Christlike attributes, and the knowledge and testimony he had acquired and cultivated.

Our Father will not force us to love Him or to follow His Son. He will not force us to obey or learn about Him. He will not force us to choose to return and live with Him. Our agency is far too important to Him.

For one reason or another, I have spent a fair amount of time in recent years talking with individuals who are struggling with their testimonies. At the risk of oversimplifying the earnest struggle or seeking of any sincere person, may I say that often the root cause of the confusion some have about the gospel comes from the combination of a steady diet of the philosophies of the world juxtaposed against a superficial understanding of the gospel. That combination is spiritually deadly. But it is a combination that can develop easily.

Our Father will not force us to love Him or to follow His Son.

The world is noisy, entertaining, and easily accessible. Most of us carry with us some kind of device that can interrupt us constantly and download anything, anywhere, anytime. But things of the Spirit come more quietly, often in solitude, and typically over a period of time after much supplication. They tend to take work and time. There is a simple reason for this:

Conversion requires immersion. Immersion in truth. Immersion in the word of God. Immersion in the teachings of prophets, seers, and revelators. And immersion in the Spirit.

True conversion doesn't just happen. It takes sustained spiritual work, and it takes desire. What do you and I really want?

When life starts to crowd in around me, I try to ask myself that question: What do I really want and hope for long-term?

I really do want to be exalted. I don't want to run the risk of living forever without the people I love and care about. That wouldn't be heaven. I don't want to face the agony of knowing I could have had all the privileges our Father has offered us but I chose to care more about something temporary and less important. I don't want to "settle" for something less. I want to be in the presence of the Father and the Son and be able to learn from Them forever. I want to learn to access fully the enabling power of the Atonement to help me continually repent so I don't have to pay for my own sins. I want to keep learning and growing rather than be stopped in my progression. I want to learn more and more and more about what the Lord has offered us through holy ordinances found only in His house. As flawed as I am, and as difficult as it seems some days to even consider what could lie ahead, I want to eventually become what our Father has said we can become.

Conversion requires immersion.

Understanding who we are, why we are here, where we may ultimately go, and what our Father has given us in terms of knowledge and privileges and power is a vital key. It is a key to dwelling with God in "never-ending happiness,"[3] and it is a key to having the influence we are capable of having forever!

THE INFLUENCE OF CONVERTED WOMEN

Women who are truly converted to the gospel of Jesus Christ, who have been endowed with power and learned how to draw upon that power, can change the world. This is not hyperbole.

President Thomas S. Monson has said that "try as some of us may, we cannot escape the influence our lives have upon the lives of others. Ours is the opportunity to build, to lift, to inspire, and indeed to lead."[4] As discussed earlier, we each have a divine errand, a mission to perform in mortality. And when we are on that errand, we are far more likely to have the influence our Father wants and needs us to have.

Latter-day Saint women have proven time and again that converted, covenant-keeping women live for something greater than themselves. They will work harder and longer for what they believe or who they love than they will ever work for themselves. There are countless examples of this from our history, but I will cite just two.

Mary Fielding Smith, widow of the martyred Hyrum, joined the Saints in their exodus from Nauvoo and was determined to go west. She was assigned to a company, but her provisions were so meager that C. Peter Lott, the captain of her company, pronounced her unprepared, claimed she would never make it with her oxen and scanty supplies, told her she would be a burden on the company, and advised her to return to Winter Quarters until she could get help. Mary responded by declaring that she would beat the captain to the Valley, and without any help from him.

Women who are truly converted to the gospel of Jesus Christ, who have been endowed with power and learned how to draw upon that power, can change the world. This is not hyperbole.

One day along the trail, true to the captain's predictions, one of Mary's best oxen lay down in its yoke, rolled over, and stiffened out his legs in dying fashion. Upon seeing the situation, the captain in essence muttered a "Told you so!" and rode off.

Undaunted, Mary believed that faith and priesthood power could move not only mountains but worn-out oxen. She located the consecrated oil she had tucked carefully inside her wagon and asked her brother Joseph Fielding to administer to the ox. Joseph poured "a portion of oil on the top of his head . . . and all laid hands upon [the ox], and one prayed, administering the ordinance as they would have done to a human being that was sick. In a moment the ox gathered up his legs, and at the first word arose to his feet, and traveled right off as well as ever."[5] Mary's faith in priesthood authority solved the problem.

Though she encountered other setbacks along the way, Mary persistently met them head-on. On the last major mountain of the journey, her team moved ahead of the company and, as promised, arrived twenty hours *ahead* of the captain.

Mary lived only four more years. But in her relatively short life, she managed to get her young son, Joseph F. Smith, to the Salt Lake Valley.

Years later, the importance of her faithful sacrifice and the reach of her influence would become obvious, as Mary's son would be ordained the sixth President of the Church and her grandson, Joseph Fielding Smith, the tenth President of the Church.

Like so many other LDS women before her and since, Mary Fielding Smith modeled the characteristics that converted, covenant-keeping women inevitably display: the desire to care for others, the talent to persevere and persuade, and the gifts of courage and heroic faith.

Belle Spafford, the ninth general president of the Relief Society, embodied those same qualities. Mayola Miltenberger, who for many years served as secretary to the Relief Society general presidency, described an experience demonstrating the kind of influence Sister Spafford routinely had. This interaction occurred at meetings of the National Council of Women:

"I recall being with Sister Spafford in a large Eastern city at a meeting [when] she was a member of the executive committee. The room was filled with distinguished women, each of whom was a strong, articulate leader in her own right. A particularly thorny and difficult issue was being debated heatedly. Finally, the presiding officer turned to President Spafford and asked her to voice an opinion on the problem. In her thoughtful, measured way, Sister Spafford analyzed the matter, stating the issue fairly, without rancor or confrontation, and offering, at the same time, reasonable options that could be accepted by all present. After a few moments' silence, one of those present rose and in a subdued voice said, 'What Mrs. Spafford has just proposed calls to my mind our insignia [a lighted candle with the words 'Lead Kindly Light' written in the smoke trail]. We have today been led by the 'kindly light' of Belle S. Spafford."[6]

President Gordon B. Hinckley spoke about the kind of influence Mary Fielding Smith, Belle Spafford, and countless Latter-day Saint women before and since have had and should continue to have: "It is not enough just to be good. You must be good for something. You must contribute good to the world. The world must be a better place for your presence. And the good that is in you must be spread to others. I do not suppose that any of us here this day will be remembered a thousand years from now. . . . But in this world so filled with problems, so constantly threatened by dark and evil challenges, you can and must rise above mediocrity, above indifference. You can become involved and speak with a strong voice for that which is right. . . . You cannot be indifferent to this great cause . . . which is the cause of Christ. You cannot simply stand on the sidelines and watch the play between the forces of good and evil."[7]

"It is not enough just to be good. You must be good for something. You must contribute good to the world. The world must be a better place for your presence. And the good that is in you must be spread to others."

—PRESIDENT GORDON B. HINCKLEY

I repeat that the Lord is going to come again. Only He knows what lies in the path between now and that millennial day. He has told us through His servants, however, that the role women will play is crucial to the unfolding of this spectacular ending drama.

More than thirty years have passed since President Spencer W. Kimball made a statement that the women of the Church have been quoting ever since: "Much of the major growth that is coming to the Church in the last days will come because many of the good women of the world (in whom there is often such an inner sense of spirituality) will be drawn to the Church in large numbers. This will happen to the degree that the women of the Church reflect righteousness and articulateness in their lives and to the degree that the women of the Church are seen as distinct and different—in happy ways—from the women of the world. . . . Thus it will be that the female exemplars of the Church will be a significant force in both the numerical and the spiritual growth of the Church in the last days."[8]

We have our work cut out for us. Said Elder Neal A. Maxwell: "It is precisely because the daughters of Zion are so uncommon that the adversary will not leave them alone."[9]

We may wonder how the Lord thinks we can possibly stand up to the forces of evil so prevalent around us and ultimately triumph in a showdown with the world. But God has never done things like man does them. He allowed Sarah to bear Isaac when she was past age, "because she judged him faithful who had promised."[10] He positioned Esther so that she could save her people. He sent Nephi back to Jerusalem with his older brothers to retrieve the plates of brass, a task that should have required a small army to accomplish. He and His Son appeared to a fourteen-year-old boy in an obscure grove of trees to commence the Restoration. God's ways are not man's ways. He "hath chosen the weak things of the world to confound the things which are mighty."[11] Elder Russell M. Nelson said it well: "The Lord uses the unlikely to accomplish the impossible."[12]

As the Apostle Paul counseled the Hebrews, it is time to "lay aside every weight [the weight of a preoccupation with the world, the weight of appearance, the weight of social pressure, the weight of comparing ourselves with each other, the weight of judging, the weight of refusing to forgive or seek forgiveness], and the sin which doth so easily beset us [precisely because we are in the process of overcoming the natural woman and coming out of the world], and let us run with patience the race that is set before us [we can't run the race of the world, the rat race, the race for fame or popularity, the race for riches, but the race set before us as women of God]."[13]

I believe that the moment we learn to unleash the full influence of converted, covenant-keeping women, the kingdom of God will change overnight. There will be more worthy couples sealed in the temple who forge ahead with strength and unity. There will be more children born in the covenant. There will be more virtuous women and men and more virtuous youth. More confidence by men, women, and children that they can hear the voice of the Spirit and receive revelation. More teenagers finding ways to serve others rather than being mesmerized by a steady diet of entertainment. More women and men and youth doing family history research. More prospective elders ordained to the Melchizedek Priesthood. More worthy missionaries preaching the gospel with power and authority. More temple work and worship. More confidence in sharing who we are and what we believe with others, particularly those not of our faith. More members helping to find investigators for missionaries to teach in their homes. More visiting teaching and home teaching that makes a difference. More conviction about holding firm to our beliefs while loving others who see the world differently and honoring their right to do so. More capacity to discern between right and wrong, between truth and error. More righteous influence in families, in communities, throughout the Church, and in the world.

> *I believe that the moment we learn to unleash the full influence of converted, covenant-keeping women, the kingdom of God will change overnight.*

WHAT I DON'T KNOW AND WHAT I DO

There are many things I do not know. I don't know why some find it easy to believe in God the Father and His Beloved Son Jesus Christ and others struggle to make sense of spiritual things. I don't know why some learn the lessons of eternity because their prayers are *not* answered as they desire and others because they *are*. I don't know why some plead with the Lord for decades for a husband and family while others seem to marry easily and some of them more than once. I don't know why some couples have children without difficulty and why other equally desiring couples struggle and plead and pray, but to no avail. I don't know why some go through life surrounded by large families and groups of friends and others' lives are marked by loneliness. I don't know why some lives are characterized by comfort and privilege and others have a constant struggle just providing daily bread. I don't know why some are plagued with one health problem after another and expend enormous energy just staying alive and others have remarkable health without doing much of anything. I don't know why the Lord has been explicit about some doctrine while making other principles and pearls of heavenly knowledge available only to sincere seekers through personal revelation.

There are, however, many things that I do know—some through experience and observation; others through immersing myself in the word of God, worshiping in the temple, and studying the teachings of prophets, seers, and revelators; and others still through personal revelation.

I know that women have a divine endowment from God and are mission-critical to the fulfillment of the plan of salvation and to building up the kingdom of God. Evidence of this can be found in every country where the Church is organized.

I know that a woman's greatest influence and power come from being pure, from obeying the teachings of Jesus Christ, from being true to her divine nature, and from learning how to access the power of God.

I know that a woman's greatest influence and power come from purity, from being true to her divine nature, and from learning how to access the power of God.

I have met and learned from women around the world and witnessed firsthand the inestimable scope of their influence. I have heard them teach and testify, observed their efforts to help the abused and comfort the forlorn, and watched them organize with lightning speed in the aftermath of disasters and provide untiring service to neighbors and friends. I have seen them spend hours comforting those in distress. I have seen them trek with youth, dragging themselves over Rocky Ridge (literally and figuratively) and sitting around smoky campfires testifying to youth that a virtuous life is a happier life. I've watched them dream up one imaginative way after another to engage six-year-olds in a gospel discussion and prod their teenage sons to finish their Eagle projects and Duty to God awards. I have seen young-adult-age women hold fast to their convictions even when it threatens or diminishes their social life. I know single mothers who have relied on help from heaven to fill the roles of father and mother in establishing a gospel-centered home. I have watched women age, lose their companions, and devote their golden—and sometimes alone—years to serving others. And I have witnessed the deep faith and sensitivity to things of the Spirit of so many female exemplars and role models.

I know women who walk miles along dusty roads to meet with priesthood leaders just to renew their temple recommends, even though there isn't a temple within a thousand miles, and walk those same roads again to check on their sisters in the spirit of watch care. I know other women who take a mind-boggling sequence of buses and subways across congested metropolitan areas just to get to church. And I know women who have recognized and accepted the gospel though it meant severe criticism and sometimes alienation from loved ones.

I have been inspired by the music, art, and writings women have created to express their testimonies, love of family, and reverence for life. I've been motivated by those working to stem the tide against threats to religious liberty. I know women who are among the best educated in the world and who use their skills to teach, enlighten, and inspire. I've heard women stand in worldwide forums, declare that there actually *is* such a thing as right and wrong, and rally their families to stand for truth and righteousness.

I have witnessed firsthand the sacrifice, sheer work, and sometimes thankless effort mothers and grandmothers, aunts and sisters, teachers and friends are willing to expend for those they love and for those whose well-being has been placed in their care.

The Savior said that we would recognize and know His followers by their fruits.[14] I am an eyewitness to the fruits of the gospel of Jesus Christ as played out in the lives of the women of the Church. I have seen that the gospel of Jesus Christ, when lived by a woman, transforms her into a woman of God—because the gospel is about change. The temple is about change. Conversion is about change.

From day one, the women of this dispensation have been pivotal to the onward rolling of the gospel kingdom. In families, communities, and the Church at large, they have been a bulwark against the adversary time and time again.

But is it time to ask ourselves, Can we do more for the Lord?

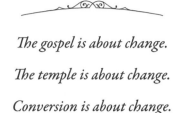

The gospel is about change.

The temple is about change.

Conversion is about change.

AS MUCH AS WE CAN

Of all the lessons President Gordon B. Hinckley taught us during his ninety-seven and a half years of living, there is a final lesson to be learned, one demonstrated during the last few years of his life. During my many interviews with him while writing his biography, it became apparent that there were really only two things he feared: getting cancer and losing his wife, Sister Marjorie Pay Hinckley. His mother had died of cancer when he was a young man, a sister had died of cancer, and a brother had died of cancer. He feared cancer. And Sister Hinckley was the love, the joy, and the emotional spark plug of his life. He couldn't imagine life without her.

Sister Hinckley did not attend the April 2004 general conference. Her absence was a first. In his concluding remarks at the conference, President Hinckley explained it by telling Church members that she was not well, that her "clock [was] winding down, and we do not know how to rewind it." He went on to say: "It is a somber time for me. We have been married for 67 years this month. She is the mother of our five gifted and able children, the grandmother of 25 grandchildren and a growing number of great-grandchildren. We've walked together side by side through all of these years, coequals and companions through storm and sunshine."[15]

Two days later, on April 6, 2004, Sister Hinckley slipped through the veil.

In the October general conference six months later, President Hinckley spoke about the "women in our lives," beginning with a tribute to his beloved wife: "My children and I were at her bedside as she slipped peacefully into eternity. As I held her hand and saw mortal life drain from her fingers, I confess I was overcome. Before I married her, she had been the girl of my dreams, to use the words of a song then popular. She was my dear companion for more than two-thirds of a century, my equal before the Lord, really my superior. And now in my old age, she has again become the girl of my dreams."[16]

The loss of Sister Hinckley was heartbreaking. But if that weren't enough, nine months later President Hinckley was diagnosed with the disease he had dreaded most of his life—cancer. He underwent surgery, but the cancer had spread. He was ninety-five years old, and most who knew President Hinckley wondered if he would live out his final days without submitting to any kind of aggressive treatment. But when he asked his doctors if they could administer chemotherapy to someone his age, and if it would extend his life, they agreed to try.

One might wonder why he didn't take the onset of cancer as an indication that his life was nearly over and the time had come to be reunited with his dear Marjorie. But he explained to those close to him, in words to this effect, "I feel I should do all I can to live as long as I can. Then when death strikes, I will know it is the Lord's will. I will know I did all that I could do."

President Hinckley lived two years from the time of his original diagnosis, likely twelve to eighteen months longer than he would have otherwise. On January 27, 2008, he passed away.

In this final act of devotion to the Lord, President Hinckley set a pattern for all of us. He demonstrated that, above all, he was determined to do *all* the Lord had sent him here to do. He modeled the admonition he had given the entire Church when he said: "We are all in this together. . . .

Within your sphere of responsibility you have as serious an obligation as do I within my sphere of responsibility. Each of us should be determined to build the kingdom of God on the earth and to further the work of righteousness."[17]

President Hinckley did as much as he could, for as long as he could.

WE ARE ALL ENLISTED

That is the challenge for each of us—to do as much as we can for the Lord, for as long as we can.

This is not to say that doing as much as we can for as long as we can is easy, because it isn't. It requires consecration and devotion. It requires true conversion. It requires us to keep going even when, *perhaps especially when,* the disappointments and curveballs of life take us places we didn't expect or want to go.

There isn't much about my life that I expected or that I have hoped and prayed for. But there is one thing I've learned through life's ups and downs: The only things that really matter are the things that matter to the Lord. Awards and plaques collect dust. Jobs change and sometimes go away. Titles and callings change. Bank accounts go up and down and sometimes disappear. But our Father and His Son do not change. Who we are doesn't change. Why we are here doesn't change. And what is important to our lives now and forever doesn't and won't change.

In this final act of devotion to the Lord, President Hinckley set a pattern for all of us. He demonstrated that, above all, he was determined to do all the Lord had sent him here to do.

He did as much as he could, for as long as he could.

What, then, are you and I to do?

A testimony is a wonderful starting point. But it is only a beginning. A testimony, or belief, that the Church is true will not be enough to see us through in the days ahead. It won't be enough to sustain our own lives, let alone enough to allow others to see the light of the gospel shining through us. As President Henry B. Eyring has taught: "Great faith has a short shelf life."[18]

Conversion requires immersion. Immersion in truth. Immersion in the scriptures. Immersion in the temple. Immersion through fasting, prayer, and time to contemplate the things of heaven.

> *The only things that really matter are the things that matter to the Lord.*

We need to think about the Lord more. We need to seek to understand who He is and what He taught.

The more we know about the Lord Jesus Christ, the more we will want to know. The more we testify about what we know, the more it will become integral to who we are.

THIS IS NOT ABOUT DOING MORE

Immersing ourselves in the things of heaven is not about doing more. But it may be about doing things differently. It is definitely about covenant making and covenant keeping. It is about immersing ourselves in the gospel of Jesus Christ so that the Spirit testifies to our spirits in such sustained, penetrating ways that we no longer question, no longer doubt, and no longer entertain temptations to hold back from full commitment to the Lord and His work.

President Harold B. Lee told about a young LDS soldier who served during World War II in England. One night he went to an officer's club where the entertainment and activities became increasingly "riotous." He noticed, however, a British officer who wasn't participating in the vulgarities. When he approached the officer and asked him why he didn't seem to be enjoying himself, the man responded, "No, sir, I can't engage in this kind of party, because, you see, I belong to the royal household of England."

As the LDS soldier walked away, he said to himself, "Neither can

I, because I belong to the royal household of the kingdom of God." President Lee then pleaded with us to be "loyal to that royal lineage" we have as members of the Church and kingdom of God.[19]

This is the crux of the matter facing each of us. Will we be loyal to who we are? Will we be loyal to our endowment as latter-day women of God?

Elder M. Russell Ballard illuminated how vital the voices of women are in defending and building the kingdom of God: "None of us can afford to stand by and watch the purposes of God be diminished and pushed aside. I invite particularly you sisters . . . throughout the Church to seek the guidance of heaven in knowing what you can do to let your voice of faith and testimony be heard. The Brethren of the General Authorities and the sisters who are general officers cannot do it alone. The full-time missionaries cannot do it alone.

Will we be loyal to who we are? Will we be loyal to our endowment as latter-day women of God?

Priesthood leaders and auxiliary leaders cannot do it alone. We must all defend our Father in Heaven and His plan. We must all defend our Savior and testify that He is the Christ, that His Church has been restored to the earth, that there is such a thing as right and wrong."[20]

I am convinced that women hold an exalted position in the eyes of the Lord. And as latter-day women of God, we have been given divine errands that include—for every one of us—defending and sustaining the kingdom of God. I know that is true.

I also know that our Father expects His daughters to learn to receive revelation.

I know that our Father and His Son are perfect and that Jesus Christ stands at the head of His Church.

I know that women are vital to the success of the Lord's Church.

I know that endowed, covenant-keeping women have access to the power of God for their personal lives.

I know that the high privilege of motherhood has been reserved for women.

I know that converted women—individually and collectively—can literally change the world.

Most of all, I know that Jesus Christ is our Savior, the Eternal Healer, and our Advocate with our Father.

I haven't received everything I've prayed for. I've had my share of disappointments. All of my worries and failings, weaknesses and anxieties haven't been magically swept away. But the Lord has never let me down, and He has never left me utterly alone.

I have lived now for six decades. During that time, I have had privileges and joys I didn't expect and certainly didn't deserve, and I have faced disappointments and heartaches that have nearly crushed me. I have had the rare privilege of sitting at the feet of prophets, and I have also been blessed with the chance to rub shoulders with and learn from a long list of magnificent women whose examples and testimonies have buoyed me up and helped me see what the women of God look like, how they handle themselves, and the way they follow the Master. Through it all, in quiet moments as well as in the midst of large congregations, I have caught spiritual glimpses of the role and majesty of women in the eyes of the Lord.

President Spencer W. Kimball declared that "to be a righteous woman is a glorious thing in any age. To be a righteous woman during the

> *I haven't received everything I've prayed for. I've had my share of heartbreaks and disappointments. All of my worries and failings and anxieties haven't been magically swept away. But the Lord has never let me down, and He has never left me utterly alone.*

winding-up scenes on this earth, before the second coming of our Savior, is an especially noble calling. The righteous woman's strength and influence today can be tenfold what it might be in more tranquil times."[21] I know this is true.

These *are* the winding-up scenes.

If it ever was easy or comfortable being a Latter-day Saint, those days are likely over. But as latter-day women of God, we *do* have an especially noble calling and a work to do.

We have not been asked to store wheat, as were our sisters of yesteryear. We have not been required to pull handcarts over Rocky Ridge. But we have been asked to store faith. We have been asked to be pure in a world that increasingly mocks purity. We have been asked to increase our capacity to receive revelation and pull down the power from heaven that God has granted His endowed sisters. We have been asked to model how women of God look and act—not only as beacons for the rising generation but for all of the house of Israel. We have been asked to stand tall and stand together in speaking for what we know to be true and right and divine.

Our influence today can be greater than the influence of any group of women in the history of the world.

The time has come for us to do things we have never done before. It is time to live up to the confidence that our Father demonstrated in us by sending us to earth now, when everything is on the line. May we immerse ourselves in the gospel of Jesus Christ until our conversion is full, complete, and ongoing. May we continue to grow in truth and knowledge, with the understanding that the more we know, the more our Father can use us to bless others. May we do as Moroni implored and "seek this Jesus of whom the prophets and apostles have written."[22] In doing so, may we seek to fully understand what Eliza R. Snow meant when she declared that we "have greater and higher privileges than any other females upon the face of the earth."[23]

I stand with Eliza. We do indeed have greater and higher privileges than any other females upon the face of this earth. Even with a lifetime of seeking, we won't plumb the depths of the power and privileges our Father has given us. It is because of our access to that power that converted women can change the world—one woman, one marriage, one family, one follower and servant of Jesus Christ at a time.

Converted women can change the world—one woman, one marriage, one family, one follower and servant of Jesus Christ at a time.

We need the help of heaven. But we have the help of heaven if we seek and learn to receive the power our Father has given us.

May we spend whatever time and make whatever effort is required to understand what our Father has given us. May we do as much as we can, for as long as we can. And then, bolstered by a confidence born of the Spirit of the Lord, may we go forth as the covenant daughters of the Lord, scattered upon all the face of the earth, armed both with righteousness and with the power of God in great glory.

JOURNAL SECTION

The Lord has said that those who receive what He has given us will receive more. Prophets, seers, and revelators have taught that when we record the insights we receive as we study the gospel, they will become more clear to us, more likely to become a permanent part of our understanding and knowledge, and more likely to bless us. These pages are provided as a convenience to capture your impressions as you seek for greater light and truth.

SHERI DEW

Women Have a Divine Errand

God Expects Women to Receive Revelation

God Is Perfect and So Is His Son

Women Are Vital to the Success of the Lord's Church

Both Women and Men Have Access to
God's Highest Spiritual Blessings

God Reserved the High Privilege of
Motherhood for Women

Converted Women Can Change the World

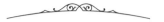

WOMEN HAVE A DIVINE ERRAND

GOD EXPECTS WOMEN
TO RECEIVE REVELATION

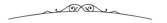

GOD IS PERFECT AND
SO IS HIS SON

WOMEN ARE VITAL TO THE SUCCESS OF THE LORD'S CHURCH

BOTH WOMEN AND MEN HAVE ACCESS TO GOD'S HIGHEST SPIRITUAL BLESSINGS

GOD RESERVED THE HIGH PRIVILEGE OF MOTHERHOOD FOR WOMEN

CONVERTED WOMEN CAN CHANGE THE WORLD

NOTES

Introduction

1. Title IX is a portion of the Education Amendments of 1972. It reads in part that "no person in the United States shall, on the basis of sex, be excluded from participation in, be denied the benefits of, or be subjected to discrimination under any education program or activity receiving federal financial assistance."
2. "Study of Active LDS Women," conducted by Deseret Book Company, 2013.
3. See Wendy Watson Nelson, *Change Your Questions, Change Your Life* (2009), for a rich understanding of the manner in which questions can lead to important answers.
4. Wilford Woodruff, in *Journal of Discourses*, 26 vols. (1856–1886), 24:54–55.
5. Wallace Stegner, *The Gathering of Zion: The Story of the Mormon Trail* (1971), 13.
6. *In Their Own Words: Women and the Story of Nauvoo* (1994), 213. Elder John A. Widtsoe elaborated on the women of the early days of the Restoration: "Woman faced the tribulations without hesitation; and perhaps she accepted the heavier part. She met with high-flung disdain the horrors of the Missouri persecutions. She crossed the frozen Missouri towards the unknown wilderness without looking back at her happy Nauvoo home from which she had been driven. On the westward trail, sheltered thinly in a wagon box from the raging blizzard, she bore her children. She toiled undismayed across the dreary desert to find a hoped-for safe haven in distant mountain valleys. With tearful eyes, but with an unquenchable faith in the unfolding of God's eternal plan, she saw her child or husband laid away in a

soon-to-be obliterated grave by a desert trail. With uncomplaining fortitude she shouldered her part of the burden of conquering the wilderness, of making the desert blossom as the rose" ("The 'Mormon' Woman," *Relief Society Magazine,* June–July 1943, 374).

7. Eliza R. Snow, "Sketch," in Maureen Ursenbach Beecher, ed., *The Personal Writings of Eliza Roxcy Snow* (2000), 21.

8. Neylan McBaine, ed., *Sisters Abroad: Interviews from the Mormon Woman Project* (2013), 32.

Chapter 1: The Question of Perception

1. Mary Zeiss Stange, "Do Women Have a Prayer?" *USA Today,* 23 March 2009.

2. Robert D. Putnam and David E. Campbell, *American Grace: How Religion Divides and Unites Us* (2010), 235, 603, n. 14.

3. Putnam and Campbell, *American Grace,* 242.

4. In July 1848, a two-day women's rights convention was held in Seneca Falls, New York. Prominent among its speakers were Lucretia Mott and Elizabeth Cady Stanton, who would become renowned voices in the push for women's suffrage in the United States. A "Declaration of Sentiments," patterned after the Declaration of Independence, laid out the issues faced by women and became a foundational document in the women's rights movement.

5. See www.lds.org.

6. See Dallin H. Oaks, "Followers of Christ," *Ensign,* May 2013, 98.

7. Sally Denton, "A Male-Dominated World," NYTimes.com, 1 January 2012.

8. Remarks, National Press Club, 8 March 2000; quoted in *Discourses of Gordon B. Hinckley,* 2 vols. (2004–5), 2:460.

9. D&C 25:7.

10. D&C 25:16; emphasis added.

11. Quoted in Sarah M. Kimball, "Auto-biography," *Woman's Exponent,* 1 September 1883, 51; see also *Teachings of Presidents of the Church: Joseph Smith* (2007), 451.

12. *History of the Church of Jesus Christ of Latter-day Saints,* 7 vols. (1932–1952), 4:602.

13. Quoted in Kimball, "Auto-biography," 51; see also *Teachings of Presidents of the Church: Joseph Smith,* 451.

14. Joseph F. Smith, *Gospel Doctrine: Selections from the Sermons and Writings of Joseph F. Smith,* ed. John A. Widtsoe (1939), 581–82.

15. Bruce R. McConkie, *Doctrines of the Restoration* (1989), 197–98; see also D&C 138:38–39.

16. *Improvement Era,* March 1942, 161.

17. James E. Faust, "What It Means to Be a Daughter of God," *Ensign,* November 1999, 101.

18. Boyd K. Packer, "The Relief Society," *Ensign,* May 1998, 73.

19. Gordon B. Hinckley, "Daughters of God," *Ensign,* November 1991, 98–99.

20. Gordon B. Hinckley, *One Bright Shining Hope* (2006), 1. President

Howard W. Hunter was glowing in his assessment of the spiritual strengths of women, saying that a woman has a "superior spirituality in the marriage relationship, and the opportunity to encourage, uplift, teach, and be the one who sets the example in the family for righteous living. When women come to the point of realizing that it is more important to be superior than to be equal, they will find the real joy in living those principles that the Lord set out in his divine plan" (*The Teachings of Howard W. Hunter,* ed. Clyde Williams [1997], eBook edition).

21. Thomas S. Monson, "Three Goals to Guide You," *Ensign,* November 2007, 120.

22. Eliza R. Snow, in Relief Society Minutes, Fifteenth Ward, Salt Lake Stake, 6 January 1870 (Church History Library), 140.

23. "Mormon Women in Council," *New York Herald,* 23 January 1870, quoted in *Deseret News,* 16 February 1870, 23.

24. Quoted in Eliza R. Snow, "An Address," *Woman's Exponent,* 15 September 1873, 63.

25. The Young Ladies Mutual Improvement Association was the forerunner of the Young Women organization.

26. *Woman's Exponent,* 1 April 1888, 165.

27. Emmeline B. Wells, "Report of the Dedication of the Kaysville Relief Society House," *Woman's Exponent,* 1 March 1877, 149.

28. See Jill Mulvay Derr, Janath Russell Cannon, and Maureen Ursenbach Beecher, *Women of Covenant: The Story of Relief Society* (1992), 208–11.

29. Quoted in James E. Talmage, "The Women's Relief Society," *Relief Society Magazine* 6 (1919): 565–67.

30. See the obituary of Ida Elizabeth Bowman Smith, *Deseret News,* late September 1918. Ida Smith is the grandmother of Elder M. Russell Ballard of the Quorum of the Twelve Apostles.

31. *Deseret News,* 11 August 1869.

32. D. Todd Christofferson, "The Power of Covenants," *Ensign,* May 2009, 19–20.

33. "The Women of Christchurch, New Zealand," video produced by Deseret Book for the BYU Women's Conference Concert, 2012. In possession of the author.

34. "Female Relief Society," *Deseret News,* 22 April 1868; quoted in *Daughters in My Kingdom: The History and Work of Relief Society* (2011), 1.

Chapter 2: Women Have a Divine Errand

1. Transcript of Mike Wallace interview with Gordon B. Hinckley, 18 December 1995, in possession of author; quoted in Sheri L. Dew, *Go Forward with Faith* (1996), 541.

2. Theaetetus 176a, trans. M. J. Levett, rev. Myles F. Burnyeat, in *Plato: Complete Works,* ed. John M. Cooper (1997), 195.

3. Irenaeus, *Adversus Haereses,* book 4, chapter 38, in *The Apostolic Fathers,*

Justin Martyr, Irenaeus, vol. 1 of *Ante-Nicene Fathers: The Writings of the Fathers Down to A. D. 325,* ed. Alexander Roberts and James Donaldson (1994), 522. The Gospel of Philip, an apocryphal book, sizes up our potential in a more pragmatic fashion: "A horse sires a horse, a man begets man, a god brings forth a god" ("The Gospel of Philip (IIc)," in *The Nag Hammadi Library: In English,* trans. Members of the Coptic Gnostic Library Project of the Institute for Antiquity and Christianity [1977], 145).

4. C. S. Lewis, *Mere Christianity* (HarperCollins, 2001), 199.

5. C. S. Lewis, *The Weight of Glory and Other Addresses* (Macmillan, n.d.), 14–15. There are admittedly those who take exception with the notion that man may become a god. Many who reject this doctrine call it blasphemy. But Brigham Young explained that "[Man's godhood] will not detract anything from the glory and might of our heavenly Father, for he will still remain our Father, and we shall still be subject to him, and as we progress, in glory and power it the more enhances the glory and power of our heavenly father" (in *Journal of Discourses,* 10:5).

6. President Henry B. Eyring referred to "divine errands" in "Where Is the Pavilion?" *Ensign,* November 2012, 74.

7. Spencer W. Kimball, "The Role of Righteous Women," *Ensign,* November 1979, 102.

8. Acts 9:1.

9. Acts 9:15; see also Acts 22:14.

10. See Acts 9:13.

11. "Winston Churchill and the Human Potential," *Saturday Review,* 6 February 1965, 18.

12. "The Parable of BYU–Hawaii," BYU–Hawaii commencement address, 17 December 2011.

13. Mosiah 2:41.

14. Romans 8:16–17.

15. Psalm 82:6.

16. Romans 8:16–17.

17. Philippians 3:14.

18. Office Journal of Lorenzo Snow, 8 October 1900 (Church History Library), 181–82.

19. Lorenzo Snow, in Conference Report, April 1901, 3.

20. Joseph F. Smith, quoted in Orson F. Whitney, *Saturday Night Thoughts,* "Article Thirty-eight," Forgotten Classics eBook edition (2010).

21. Dallin H. Oaks, "The Great Plan of Happiness," *Ensign,* November 1993, 72.

22. About the transition from this life to the next, or death, Elder Melvin J. Ballard explained: "We will never appreciate the value of this mortal body until we lose it. But when we do lose it, we will discover that we are entities just as real as we are here and now. . . . We will be so real that it will take some of us days to convince ourselves we are dead, when we have separated from the body; and not until we turn to do what we used to do while in the

body, and cannot do it, will it dawn upon us that we are dead, or that we are separated from the body, and then we will look forward in great anticipation to the day of resurrection when the body and the spirit can be reunited once again, never to be parted" (*Sermons and Missionary Services of Melvin J. Ballard,* comp. Bryant S. Hinckley [1949], 180).

23. *Gospel Truth: Discourses and Writings of George Q. Cannon,* comp. Jerreld L. Newquist (1957), 8.

24. D&C 138:56.

25. Elder Orson F. Whitney explained that though we cannot remember definitively what happened in our premortal life, "more than once, after meeting someone whom I had never met before on earth, I have wondered why his or her face seemed so familiar. Many times, upon hearing a noble sentiment expressed, though unable to recall having heard it until then, I have been thrilled by it, and felt as if I had always known it. The same is true of music, some strains of which are like echoes from afar, sounds falling from celestial heights. . . . I do not assert pre-acquaintance in all such cases, but as one thought suggests another, these queries arise in my mind" (*Saturday Night Thoughts,* "Article Thirty-eight").

26. Joseph Smith, *Teachings of the Prophet Joseph Smith,* selected and arranged by Joseph Fielding Smith (1976), 181.

27. See Job 38:7.

28. Joseph Fielding Smith, *Doctrines of Salvation,* 3 volumes (1954–1956), 1:58–59.

29. Revelation 12:7–9.

30. *Gospel Truth,* 7.

31. William Wordsworth, "Ode on Intimations of Immortality."

32. John 10:27.

33. Elder Orson F. Whitney asked, "Can a sheep know the voice of its shepherd, if it has never heard that voice before? They who love Truth, and to whom it appeals most powerfully, were they not its best friends in a previous state of existence? I think so. I believe that we knew the Gospel before we came here, and it is this knowledge, this acquaintance, that gives to it a familiar sound" (*Saturday Night Thoughts,* "Article Thirty-eight").

34. Tad R. Callister, *The Infinite Atonement* (2000), 181.

35. D&C 33:3–4.

36. Abraham 2:8.

37. *Gospel Truth,* 8.

38. *Juvenile Instructor,* 1 May 1887, 22:140.

39. *Gospel Truth,* 18. See also *Journal of Discourses,* 11:230.

40. Abraham 3:22–23.

41. D&C 138:53, 55.

42. D&C 121:28.

43. Moses 6:31.

44. Moses 7:21.

45. See Revelation 12:7–17; see also JST, Revelation 12:6–17.

46. See "Women Have Made No Progress at the Top," *USA Today,* 11 March 2013; also "I Do Not Wish That for Anyone," *Daily Mail* Online, 10 March 2013.

47. "Study Finds Movie Industry Sexualizing Women at Earlier Ages," deseretnews.com, 23 April 2011.

48. 1 Samuel 16:7.

49. Moses 1:12–13, 4–6; emphasis added.

50. Tad R. Callister, "The Power of the Priesthood in the Boy," *Ensign,* May 2013, 53.

51. Bruce R. McConkie, *A New Witness for the Articles of Faith* (1985), 513.

52. Ezra Taft Benson, "Jesus Christ—Gifts and Expectations," in *Speeches of the Year, 1974,* 313. In this regard, Brigham Young taught: "I want to tell you, each and every one of you, that you are well acquainted with God our heavenly Father, or the great Elohim . . . for there is not a soul of you but what has lived in His house and dwelt with Him year after year. . . . There is not a person here to-day but what is a son or a daughter of that Being" (in *Journal of Discourses,* 9:291).

    Victor Hugo, author of the classic *Les Miserables,* spoke with prescient foresight about the opportunities that he sensed beyond the veil: "The nearer I approach the end, the plainer I hear around me the immortal symphonies of the worlds which invite me. . . . For half a century I have been writing my thoughts in prose and verse; history. . . . I have tried all. But I feel I have not said a thousandth part of what is in me. When I go down to the grave I can say, like so many others, 'I have finished my day's work,' but I cannot say, 'I have finished my life.' My day's work will begin again the next morning. The tomb is not a blind alley; it is a thoroughfare. . . . My work is only beginning" (as related by Arsene Houssaye, "Victor Hugo on immortality," in Samuel Gordon Lathrop, ed., *Fifty Years and Beyond; or, Gathered Gems for the Aged* [1881], 325; quoted by Hugh B. Brown in Conference Report, April 1967, 50).

53. Quoted by LeGrand Richards, "I Am More Interested in the Long Hereafter than the Brief Present," BYU devotional address, 25 February 1975.

54. Spencer W. Kimball, "The Things of Eternity—Stand We in Jeopardy?" *Ensign,* January 1977, 3.

55. J. R. R. Tolkien, *The Fellowship of the Ring* (Ballantine Books, 1965), 82.

56. Joseph Fielding Smith, *Doctrines of Salvation,* 2:18–19.

57. Lewis, *Mere Christianity,* 174–75.

58. JST, Matthew 6:38.

59. M. Russell Ballard, "Here Am I, Send Me," BYU devotional address, 13 March 2001.

Chapter 3: God Expects Women to Receive Revelation

1. Henry B. Eyring, "Where Is the Pavilion?" *Ensign,* November 2012, 73.

2. Acts 20:35.

3. Mark 12:43–44.

4. See Genesis 25:22–23.

5. *Nauvoo Relief Society Minute Book,* 19 April 1842. Available online at http://josephsmithpapers.org/paperDetails/nauvoo-relief-society-minute-book.

6. Eliza R. Snow, "An Address by Miss Eliza R. Snow," *Millennial Star,* January 13, 1874, 18.

7. 2 Nephi 28:30; emphasis added.

8. Bruce R. McConkie, *A New Witness for the Articles of Faith,* 489.

9. Moroni 10:5.

10. Richard G. Scott, *21 Principles: Divine Truths to Help You Live by the Spirit* (eBook edition, 2013), "Principle 20"; emphasis added.

11. See 1 Nephi 13:37.

12. See 2 Nephi 32:2–3, 5.

13. 2 Nephi 32:7; emphasis added.

14. Heber C. Kimball, in *Journal of Discourses,* 10:167–68; emphasis added.

15. D&C 88:32–33; emphasis added.

16. *Teachings of the Prophet Joseph Smith,* 328.

17. *Teachings of the Prophet Joseph Smith,* 149.

18. See D&C 76:5–10.

19. D&C 121:26, 33.

20. Alma 42:27; emphasis added.

21. D&C 88:63.

22. D&C 42:61.

23. D&C 121:28.

24. Spencer W. Kimball, *Faith Precedes the Miracle* (1972), 65–66.

25. Bruce R. McConkie, "The Lord's People Receive Revelation," *Ensign,* June 1971, 77–78.

26. Scott, *21 Principles,* "Principle 1."

27. Spencer W. Kimball, "Privileges and Responsibilities of Sisters," *Ensign,* November 1978, 105.

28. Helaman 4:24.

29. Parley P. Pratt, *Key to the Science of Theology* (1978), 61.

30. Russell M. Nelson, "Living by Scriptural Guidance," *Ensign,* November 2000, 17.

31. Mosiah 3:19.

32. *Teachings of the Prophet Joseph Smith,* 151.

33. See Alma 32:27–28.

34. See Matthew 11:28–30; Luke 4:18; Jacob 2:8; Alma 7:11–12; Ether 12:27.

35. 2 Nephi 25:13.

36. 1 Corinthians 12:31.

37. Quoted in Marvin J. Ashton, *The Measure of Our Hearts* (1991), 24–25.

38. D&C 10:5.

39. Jacob 4:13.

40. D&C 93:24.

41. Scott, *21 Principles,* "Principle 16."
42. Email from Colette Burnham to Wendy Watson Nelson, 13 May 2013, in author's possession. Used by permission.
43. Henry B. Eyring, "Education for Real Life," CES fireside, 6 May 2001.

Chapter 4: God Is Perfect and So Is His Son

1. See "The Family: A Proclamation to the World."
2. Moses 1:39; see also Alma 42:26.
3. See Abraham 4.
4. *Cowley and Whitney on Doctrine,* comp. Forace Green [1963], 287.
5. See "The Family: A Proclamation to the World."
6. See Luke 10:42.
7. "The Family: A Proclamation to the World."
8. Hugh W. Nibley, *When the Lights Went Out: Three Studies on the Ancient Apostasy* (1970), 1.
9. As quoted in LeGrand Richards, *A Marvelous Work and a Wonder* (1958), 3–4.
10. Joseph Smith–History 1:19.
11. Gordon B. Hinckley, "The Stone Cut Out of the Mountain," *Ensign,* November 2007, 86.
12. 3 Nephi 27:8.
13. D&C 115:4.
14. In the 2013 New Mission Presidents Seminar, Elder Jeffrey R. Holland made the statement that as much as we believe in families, the Church isn't the "Church of the Happy Family," because it is The Church of Jesus Christ of Latter-day Saints.
15. Harry Emerson Fosdick, *Martin Luther* (1956), 174–75.
16. James E. Talmage, *The Great Apostasy* (1968), 158. In an effort to verify Elder Talmage's statement, Elder Tad R. Callister asked Dr. Richard Holzapfel, a professor of religious history at Brigham Young University, to search the vast archive of information now available electronically in an effort to see if he could confirm Elder Talmage's conclusion reached decades ago. Elder Callister later reported: "After extensive research [Dr. Holzapfel] wrote: 'In the USA, it seems there was no organization using any form of the Lord's name as a title for their church [before the Church was restored in 1830].' The closest names he found were (1) United Society of Believers in Christ's Second Appearing (Shakers), (2) Church of the United Brethren in Christ (German Pietistic Group), and (3) Christian Quakers and Friends. Today there are churches with Christ's or God's name, but evidently they did not appear until *after* the organization of The Church of Jesus Christ of Latter-day Saints in 1830" (Tad R. Callister, *The Inevitable Apostasy and the Promised Restoration* [2006], 291).
17. Russell M. Nelson, "How Firm Our Foundation," *Ensign,* May 2002, 75.
18. Proverbs 3:5.

19. Jacob 4:10.

20. Wilford Woodruff, in *Journal of Discourses*, 24:54–55.

21. Isaiah 55:9.

22. See Jacob 4:8.

23. See D&C 88:47.

24. Bruce R. McConkie, "The Seven Deadly Heresies," BYU devotional address, 1 June 1980.

25. See Matthew 6:8.

26. See Acts 15:18.

27. *History of the Church,* 5:135.

28. See Matthew 13:15.

29. D&C 46:13.

30. See Luke 9:1–2.

31. See James 1:5; 1 Kings 19:12; Matthew 7:7; D&C 8:2.

32. Gordon B. Hinckley, "The Marvelous Foundation of Our Faith," *Ensign*, November 2002, 80.

33. Henry B. Eyring, "Come Unto Me," *Ensign,* May 2013, 25.

34. Harold B. Lee, "Be Loyal to the Royal within You," BYU devotional address, 11 September 1973.

Chapter 5: Women Are Vital to the Success of the Lord's Church

1. Such privileges to serve, for men and women alike, come because we are called to serve, and not because we ask for or seek the privileges.

2. Regarding the organization of the Relief Society, Eliza R. Snow said that "although the name may be of modern date, the institution is of ancient origin. We were told by our martyred prophet that the same organization existed in the Church ancient" ("Female Relief Society," *Deseret News,* 22 April 1868).

3. Recorded by Sarah M. Kimball in 1882 in her capacity as general secretary of the Relief Society, as quoted in *Daughters in My Kingdom* (2011), 12.

4. *Nauvoo Relief Society Minute Book,* 17 March 1842.

5. *Nauvoo Relief Society Minute Book,* 30 March 1842.

6. D&C 107:19; 84:19.

7. "Woman's Status," *Woman's Exponent,* 15 July 1872, 29.

8. *Relief Society Magazine,* December 1945, 717.

9. See D&C 27:6; 86:10; 109:23.

10. For an understanding of the importance of the St. George Temple in the full establishment of temple ordinances, see Blaine M. Yorgason, Richard A. Schmutz, and Douglas Alder, *All That Was Promised: The St. George Temple and the Unfolding of the Restoration* (2013).

11. See 2 Nephi 2:23.

12. Dallin H. Oaks, "The Great Plan of Happiness," *Ensign,* November 1993, 73.

13. Moses 5:11.

14. James E. Faust, "What It Means to Be a Daughter of God," *Ensign,* November 1999, 101.
15. D&C 138:39.
16. Adam and Eve together "called upon the name of the Lord," "heard the voice of the Lord," "made all things known" to their children, and "ceased not to call upon God" (Moses 5:4, 12, 16).
17. Hebrews 11:11.
18. See Judges 4:4; 5:7.
19. See Esther 4:14.
20. See 1 Kings 17:10–16.
21. Alma 7:10.
22. John 4:1–14.
23. Luke 10:38–41.
24. John 11:25–27.
25. Matthew 27:55.
26. Mark 15:47.
27. See Luke 24:1, 10.
28. See Matthew 27:55–56, 61; Mark 15:40, 47; Luke 23:49, 55; 24:1–10; John 19:25–27; 20:11–18.
29. James E. Talmage, *Jesus the Christ* (1916), 475.
30. Edward W. Tullidge, *The Women of Mormondom* (1877), 76.
31. Tullidge, *Women of Mormondom,* 4–6, 107.
32. Quentin L. Cook, "LDS Women Are Incredible!" *Ensign,* May 2011, 20–21.
33. Heber J. Grant, *Gospel Standards* (1941), 150.
34. Julie B. Beck, "Why Are We Organized into Quorums and Relief Societies?" BYU devotional address, 17 January 2012.
35. Tullidge, *Women of Mormondom,* 145–46.
36. Relief Society General Board Minutes, 1914.
37. John A. Widtsoe, "The 'Mormon' Woman," *Relief Society Magazine,* June–July 1943, 372.

Chapter 6: Both Women and Men Have Access to God's Highest Spiritual Blessings

1. "The Mission of the Church and Its Members," *Improvement Era,* November 1956, 781.
2. M. Russell Ballard, "This Is My Work and Glory," *Ensign,* May 2013, 18–19.
3. 1 Nephi 14:14; emphasis added.
4. Neal A. Maxwell, "The Tugs and Pulls of the World," *Ensign,* November 2000, 35.
5. See Mosiah 18:8–10; 2 Nephi 32:2–5; D&C 109:9, 13, 15, 22; 132:19–20.
6. See 1 Nephi 13:37.
7. D&C 84:26.
8. D&C 109:15, 22.

9. Bruce R. McConkie, "Our Sisters from the Beginning," *Ensign,* January 1979, 61.

10. See D&C 107:20.

11. See D&C 107:18.

12. Dallin H. Oaks, "Priesthood Authority in the Family and the Church," *Ensign,* November 2005, 26.

13. Ballard, "This Is My Work," 19.

14. JST, Genesis 14:30–31; see also vv. 25–40.

15. Bruce R. McConkie, "The Doctrine of the Priesthood," *Ensign,* May 1982, 32; emphasis added. Elder McConkie added: "Priesthood is . . . the very power of God himself, the power by which the worlds were made, the power by which all things are regulated, upheld, and preserved. . . . It is that we have power, by faith, to govern and control all things, both temporal and spiritual; to work miracles and perfect lives; to stand in the presence of God and be like him because we have gained his faith, his perfections, and his power, or in other words the fulness of his priesthood" ("Doctrine of the Priesthood," 32, 34).

16. M. Russell Ballard, "Let Us Think Straight," BYU Campus Education Week devotional address, 20 August 2013; see also D&C 109:15, 22.

17. Tad R. Callister, "The Power of the Priesthood in the Boy," *Ensign,* May 2013, 53.

18. Boyd K. Packer, *Mine Errand from the Lord* (2009), 253.

19. M. Russell Ballard, "Here Am I, Send Me," BYU devotional address, 13 March 2001.

20. Ballard, "This Is My Work," 19.

21. Gordon B. Hinckley, "Women of the Church," *Ensign,* November 1996, 70.

22. Neal A. Maxwell, "The Women of God," *Ensign,* May 1978, 10–11.

23. Jeffrey R. Holland, "Lord, I Believe," *Ensign,* May 2013, 94; emphasis added.

24. *Nauvoo Relief Society Minute Book,* 28 April 1842. The account of the latter statement in the *History of the Church* was amplified: "President Smith then gave instruction respecting the propriety of females administering to the sick by the prayer of faith, the laying on hands, or the anointing of oil; and said it was according to revelation that the sick should be nursed with herbs and mild food. . . . Who are better qualified to administer than our faithful and zealous sisters, whose hearts are full of faith, tenderness, sympathy and compassion. No one" (*History of the Church,* 4:607).

A second example of potential confusion about women and priesthood centers around Eliza's recording that Joseph proposed to "ordain" the new Relief Society presidency to preside over the Society. Elder John Taylor later clarified that Emma did not receive priesthood keys or authority: "On the occasion of the organization of the Relief Society, by the Prophet Joseph Smith at Nauvoo, I was present Sister Emma Smith was elected president and Sisters Elizabeth Ann Whitney and Sarah M. Cleveland her Counselors. The Prophet Joseph then said that Sister Emma was named in the revelation recorded in the Book of Doctrine and Covenants concerning the Elect Lady, and furthermore that she had been ordained to expound the Scriptures. . . . The ordination then given did not mean the conferring of the Priesthood upon those sisters yet the sisters hold a portion of the Priesthood in connection with their husbands. (Sisters Eliza R. Snow and Bathsheba W. Smith, stated that they so understood it in Nauvoo and have looked upon it always in that light.) As I stated, at that meeting, I was called upon by the Prophet Joseph and I did ordain Sisters Whitney and Cleveland, and blessed Sister Emma and set her apart. I could not ordain these sisters to anything more or to greater powers than had been conferred upon Sister Emma who had previously been ordained to expound the Scriptures, and that Joseph said at that time, that being an elect lady had its significance, and that the revelation was then fulfilled in Sister Emma being thus elected to preside over the Relief Society" (*Woman's Exponent*, 1 September 1880, 53).

25. Dallin H. Oaks, "The Relief Society and the Church," *Ensign*, May 1992, 36.

26. Ordination to the priesthood is a divinely appointed, foreordained privilege and responsibility and not a license to dominate. Those ordained are given power that enables them to bless and serve in unique ways that transcend anything earthly. But the Lord has made clear the rules for exercising priesthood power. The rights to use the priesthood are "inseparably connected with the powers of heaven," and they cannot be "controlled nor handled only upon the principles of righteousness" (D&C 121:36). Leaving little to interpretation, the Lord spelled out what that means. When men attempt to cover their sins, gratify their pride or vain ambitions, or to "exercise control or dominion or compulsion upon the souls of the children of men, in *any degree of unrighteousness,* behold, the heavens withdraw themselves; the Spirit of the Lord is grieved; and when it is withdrawn, Amen to the priesthood or the authority of that man" (D&C 121:37; emphasis added).

27. Spencer W. Kimball, "Our Sisters in the Church," *Ensign,* November 1979, 49. Elder M. Russell Ballard said something similar: "There are some men, including some priesthood leaders, who have not yet seen the light and who still do not include our sister leaders in full partnership in ward and stake councils. I also acknowledge that there are some men who oppress women and in some rare circumstances are guilty of abusing women. This is abhorrent in the eyes of God. I feel certain that men who in any way demean women will answer to God for their actions. And let me add that any priesthood leader who does not involve his sister leaders with full respect and inclusion is not honoring and magnifying the keys he has been given. His power and influence will be diminished until he learns the ways of the Lord" ("Let Us Think Straight," BYU Campus Education Week devotional address, 20 August 2013).

28. Holland, "Lord, I Believe," 94.

29. Mormon 8:17.

30. D&C 107:8.

31. Callister, "Power of the Priesthood in the Boy," 52.
32. *Handbook 2: Administering the Church,* The Church of Jesus Christ of Latter-day Saints (2010), 8.
33. Oaks, "Priesthood Authority in the Family and the Church," 26.
34. *Handbook 2: Administering the Church,* 8.
35. Oaks, "The Relief Society and the Church," 36.
36. D&C 128:9–11.
37. *Handbook 2: Administering the Church,* 9.
38. *Handbook 2: Administering the Church,* 8.
39. Bruce R. McConkie, *A New Witness for the Articles of Faith* (1985), 309.
40. Boyd K. Packer, "Covenants," *Ensign,* May 1987, 24.
41. *Relief Society Magazine,* January 1965, 5.
42. *Relief Society Magazine,* January 1959, 4. Elder Dallin H. Oaks clarified that President Joseph Fielding Smith's teaching on authority "explains what the Prophet Joseph Smith meant when he said that he organized the Relief Society 'under the priesthood after the pattern of the priesthood.' The authority to be exercised by the officers and teachers of the Relief Society . . . was the authority that would flow to them through their organizational connection with The Church of Jesus Christ of Latter-day Saints and through their individual setting apart under the hands of the priesthood leaders by whom they were called" ("The Relief Society and the Church," 36.)
43. *Nauvoo Relief Society Minute Book,* 28 April 1842. Joseph Smith later described this address in these terms: "At two o'clock I met the members of the 'Female Relief Society,' and . . . gave a lecture on the Priesthood, showing how the sisters would come in possession of the privileges, blessings and gifts of the Priesthood, and that the signs should follow them, such as healing the sick, casting out devils, &c. and that they might attain unto these blessings by a virtuous life, and conversation, and diligence in keeping all the commandments" (*History of the Church,* 4:602).
44. *Nauvoo Relief Society Minute Book,* 28 April 1842.
45. See Jill Mulvay Derr, Janath Russell Cannon, and Maureen Ursenbach Beecher, *Women of Covenant: The Story of Relief Society* (1992), 47–48 for further discussion on this point.
46. Oaks, "The Relief Society and the Church," 35–36. Elder Oaks further explained that "the same is true of priesthood authority and of the related authority exercised under priesthood direction. Organizations may channel the exercise of such authority, but they do not embody it. Thus, the priesthood keys were delivered to the members of the First Presidency and the Quorum of Twelve apostles, not to any organizations" ("The Relief Society and the Church," 36).
47. About this meeting, Elder George A. Smith recorded: "[Joseph] spoke of delivering the keys of the Priesthood to the Church, and said that the faithful members of the Relief Society should receive them in connection with their husbands, that the Saints whose integrity has been tried and proved

faithful, might know how to ask the Lord and receive an answer" (*History of the Church,* 4:604).

48. "Autobiography of Sarah DeArmon Pea Rich," Church History Library; as quoted in Truman G. Madsen, *Joseph Smith the Prophet* (1989), 168–69 n. 12.

49. Spencer W. Kimball, "Relief Society—Its Promise and Potential," *Ensign,* March 1976, 2.

50. 2 Nephi 9:20.

51. *Improvement Era,* June 1970, 66.

52. *Nauvoo Relief Society Minute Book,* 28 April 1842.

53. Verses in the Doctrine and Covenants, including D&C 84:19–22, 33–40; 107:18–20; 121:26–29, 33 are excellent places to begin a study of the fruits and blessings of the Melchizedek Priesthood. In general, Sections 20, 76, 84, 107, 121, and 124 of the Doctrine and Covenants, along with Alma 13, provide an excellent curriculum.

54. D&C 107:18.

55. Said Brigham Young, "Every man and woman may be a revelator, and have the testimony of Jesus, which is the spirit of prophecy, and foresee the mind and will of God concerning them, eschew evil, and choose that which is good" *(Discourses of Brigham Young,* sel. and arr. John A. Widtsoe, [1954], 131).

56. *Evening News,* 14 January 1870.

57. D. Todd Christofferson, "The Power of Covenants," *Ensign,* May 2009, 20, 22.

58. D&C 109:15, 22.

59. *Discourses of Brigham Young,* 416.

60. *Discourses of Brigham Young,* 131.

61. D&C 76:8; 38:39; Alma 12:9.

62. John A. Widtsoe, "Temple Worship," *Utah Genealogical and Historical Magazine,* April 1921, 63.

63. *Teachings of the Prophet Joseph Smith,* Joseph Fielding Smith, comp. (1976), 149; emphasis added.

64. D&C 84:33–34.

65. D&C 84:35–40; emphasis added.

66. D&C 25:1; emphasis added.

67. 3 Nephi 9:16–17; emphasis added.

68. 1 Corinthians 11:11.

69. D&C 131:2; 132:16, 19–20.

70. See D&C 132:15–17.

71. See D&C 131:1–2.

72. John A. Widtsoe, *Priesthood and Church Government* (1962), 83; emphasis added.

73. Charles W. Penrose, in Conference Report, April 1921, 24.

74. Richard G. Scott, "The Joy of Living the Great Plan of Happiness," *Ensign,* November 1996, 73–74.

75. David A. Bednar, "We Believe in Being Chaste," *Ensign,* May 2013, 41–42.

76. James E. Talmage, *House of the Lord* (1976), 79; emphasis added.

77. 1 Peter 3:7.

78. *Young Woman's Journal,* October 1914, 602.

79. Harold B. Lee, *The Teachings of Harold B. Lee* (1996), 292.

80. Gordon B. Hinckley, "The Women in Our Lives," *Ensign,* May 2004, 84.

81. Bruce C. Hafen, "Crossing Thresholds and Becoming Equal Partners," *Ensign,* August 2007, 27.

82. Hafen, "Crossing Thresholds," 27.

83. John A. Widtsoe, *Evidences and Reconciliations* (1960), 300. About the issue of men, women, and priesthood, Elder Widtsoe also said: "Priesthood is to be used for the benefit of the entire human family, for the upbuilding of men, women and children alike. There is indeed no privileged class or sex within the true Church of Christ; and in reality there can be no discrimination between the sexes only as human beings make it or permit it" (*Priesthood and Church Government,* 92).

84. Bruce R. McConkie, "Eve and the Fall," *Woman* (1979), 68.

85. D&C 88:32–33.

86. Joseph Smith taught that "the Melchizedek Priesthood . . . is the grand head, and . . . is the channel through which all knowledge, doctrine, the plan of salvation and every important matter is revealed from heaven" (*Teachings of the Prophet Joseph Smith,* 166–67).

87. Romans 8:17.

Chapter 7: God Reserved the High Privilege of Motherhood for Women

1. In a private conversation with Dr. Truman G. Madsen in 1996, he referred to mortality as a "spook alley."

2. Jeffrey R. Holland, "'Because She Is a Mother,'" *Ensign,* May 1997, 36.

3. Heber J. Grant, *Gospel Standards* (1941), 150, 151.

4. John 19:27.

5. It is an interesting exercise to read D&C 121:40–46 and contemplate how those verses might apply to women with respect to the doctrine of motherhood.

6. Dallin H. Oaks, "The Great Plan of Happiness," *Ensign,* November 1993, 72.

7. See "The Lord's Plan for Men and Women," *Ensign,* October 1975, 4.

8. Spencer W. Kimball, "Privileges and Responsibilities of Sisters," *Ensign,* November 1978, 105.

9. As quoted in "America's Baby Bust," *Wall Street Journal,* February 2–3, 2013.

10. 2 Nephi 2:18.

11. Moses 4:26.

12. Hugh B. Brown, *Continuing the Quest* (1961), 7.

13. "The Message of the First Presidency to the Church," *Improvement Era,* November 1942, 761.

14. See Alma 13:2–4, 7–8.

15. President Spencer W. Kimball taught that the assignments of men and women differ, "with women being given the many tremendous responsibilities of motherhood and sisterhood and men being given the tremendous responsibilities of fatherhood and the priesthood—but the man is not without the woman nor the woman without the man in the Lord (see 1 Cor. 11:11)" ("The Role of Righteous Women," *Ensign,* November 1979, 102).

16. Gordon B. Hinckley, *Teachings of Gordon B. Hinckley* (1997), 387.

17. Matthew Cowley, *Matthew Cowley Speaks* (1954), 109.

18. David O. McKay, *Gospel Ideals* (1954), 453–54.

19. Russell M. Nelson, "How Firm Our Foundation," *Ensign,* May 2002, 76.

20. John A. Widtsoe, *Evidences and Reconciliations* (1960), 244; emphasis added.

21. J. Reuben Clark Jr., "Our Wives and Our Mothers in the Eternal Plan," *Relief Society Magazine,* December 1946, 801.

22. Boyd K. Packer, *The Things of the Soul* (1996), 172.

23. *Journal of Discourses,* 19:72.

24. Brown, *Continuing the Quest,* 7.

25. Abraham 3:26. Elder M. Russell Ballard taught, "Sisters, we, your brethren, cannot do what you were divinely designated to do from before the foundation of the world. We may try, but we cannot ever hope to replicate your unique gifts. There is nothing in this world as personal, as nurturing, or as life-changing as the influence of a righteous woman" ("Mothers and Daughters," *Ensign,* May 2010, 18).

26. Boyd K. Packer, *Mine Errand from the Lord* (2009), 254.

27. Boyd K. Packer, "The Work of Salvation," Worldwide Leadership Broadcast, 23 June 2013.

28. Moses 5:11.

29. Holland, "'Because She Is a Mother,'" 36. Elder Orson F. Whitney taught something similar: "The Prophet Joseph Smith declared—and he never taught more comforting doctrine—that the eternal sealings of faithful parents and the divine promises made to them for valiant service in the Cause of Truth, would save not only themselves, but likewise their posterity. Though some of the sheep may wander, the eye of the Shepherd is upon them, and sooner or later they will feel the tentacles of Divine Providence reaching out after them and drawing them back to the fold. Either in this life or the life to come, they will return. They will have to pay their debt to justice; they will suffer for their sins; and may tread a thorny path; but if it leads them at last, like the penitent Prodigal, to a loving and forgiving father's heart and home, the painful experience will not have been in vain. Pray for your careless and disobedient children; hold on to them with your faith. Hope on, trust on, till you see the salvation of God" (in Conference Report, April 1929, 110).

30. John A. Widtsoe, *Priesthood and Church Government* (1962), 85.

31. Melvin J. Ballard, *Sermons and Missionary Services of Melvin Joseph Ballard,* comp. Bryant S. Hinckley (1949), 206–7.

32. John W. Taylor, in *The Life and Labors of Eliza R. Snow Smith: with a Full Account of Her Funeral Services* (1888), 24.

33. Hebrews 12:2.

34. Henry B. Eyring, "The Enduring Legacy of Relief Society," *Ensign,* November 2009, 123–24.

35. See 2 Timothy 1:5.

36. Boyd K. Packer, "These Things I Know," *Ensign,* May 2013, 7.

37. Kieth Merrill to Sheri Dew, email correspondence, 9 March 2011.

38. Lucy Mack Smith, *The History of Joseph Smith by His Mother,* revised and enhanced edition, ed. Scot Facer Proctor and Maurine Jensen Proctor (1996), 48–50.

39. Recollection of Susa Young Gates, in *History of the Young Ladies MIA* (1911), 16.

40. "The Family: A Proclamation to the World."

41. "O My Father," *Hymns of The Church of Jesus Christ of Latter-day Saints* (1985), 292.

42. Holland, "'Because She Is a Mother,'" 36.

43. Quentin L. Cook, "LDS Women Are Incredible!" *Ensign,* May 2011, 21.

44. Spencer W. Kimball, *My Beloved Sisters* (1979), 17.

45. Proverbs 22:6.

46. See Job 38:7.

47. *Young Woman's Journal* 2 (November 1890): 81. Truman G. Madsen said that "one can refuse to bear (beget) children. And one can refuse to bear (love and nurture) begotten children. Both refusals are epidemic in our time" (*Joseph Smith the Prophet* [1989], 148 n. 24).

Chapter 8: Converted Women Can Change the World

1. Janice Kapp Perry, *The Sisters of Zion: Sister Missionary Collection,* CD released by Prime Recordings, 2013. Original version, "As Sisters in Zion," in *Hymns,* 309.

2. *Church News,* 17 February 2007.

3. Mosiah 2:41.

4. Thomas S. Monson, "Guideposts for Life's Journey," BYU devotional address, 13 November 2007.

5. Edward W. Tullidge, *The Women of Mormondom* (1877), 347–48.

6. Foreword in Belle S. Spafford, *A Woman's Reach* (1974), ii.

7. Gordon B. Hinckley, "Stand Up for Truth," BYU devotional address, 17 September 1996.

8. Spencer W. Kimball, "The Role of Righteous Women," *Ensign,* November 1979, 103–4.

9. Neal A. Maxwell, "The Women of God," *Ensign,* May 1978, 10–11. C. S. Lewis maintained that no one "knows how bad he is till he has tried very

hard to be good. A silly idea is current that good people do not know what temptation means. This is an obvious lie. Only those who try to resist temptation know how strong it is. After all, you find out the strength of the German army by fighting it, not by giving in. You find out the strength of the wind by trying to walk against it, not by lying down. A man who gives in to temptation after five minutes simply does not know what it would have been like an hour later. That is why bad people, in one sense, know very little about badness. They have lived a sheltered life by always giving in. We never find out the strength of the evil impulse inside us until we try to fight it: and Christ, because He was the only man who never yielded to temptation, is also the only man who knows to the full what temptation means—the only complete realist" *(Inspirational Writings of C. S. Lewis* [1996], 337–38).

10. Hebrews 11:11.
11. 1 Corinthians 1:27; see also D&C 35:13.
12. "Something Amazing Happened Today," *Church News,* 7 November 2009.
13. Hebrews 12:1.
14. See Matthew 7:16, 20.
15. Gordon B. Hinckley, "Concluding Remarks," *Ensign,* May 2004, 104.
16. Gordon B. Hinckley, "The Women in Our Lives," *Ensign,* November 2004, 82.
17. Gordon B. Hinckley, "An Ensign to the Nations, a Light to the World," *Ensign,* November 2003, 82.
18. Henry B. Eyring, *Choose Higher Ground* (2013), 38.
19. Harold B. Lee, "Be Loyal to the Royal within You," BYU devotional address, 11 September 1973.
20. M. Russell Ballard, "Let Us Think Straight," BYU Campus Education Week devotional address, 20 August 2013.
21. Spencer W. Kimball, *My Beloved Sisters* (1979), 17.
22. Ether 12:41.
23. *Deseret Evening News,* 15 January 1870, 2.

INDEX